Managing the
Cycle of Meltdowns
for Students with
Autism Spectrum Disorder

To my brothers Neville and Peter

We have rejoiced together on countless occasions and have buoyed each other through thick and thin—my grateful thanks to you both.

Geoff Colvin

To my wife, Liwen

For her love, support, and encouragement in this and all my life endeavors

Martin Sheehan

Managing the
Cycle of Meltdowns

for Students with

Autism Spectrum Disorder

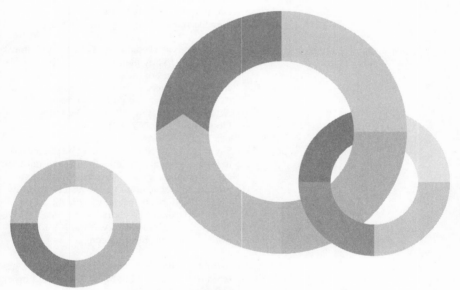

Geoff Colvin
Martin R. Sheehan

Foreword by Richard L. Simpson

Skyhorse Publishing

Skyhorse Publishing books may be purchased in bulk at special discounts for sales promotion, corporate gifts, fund-raising, or educational purposes. Special editions can also be created to specifications. For details, contact the Special Sales Department, Skyhorse Publishing, 307 West 36th Street, 11th Floor, New York, NY 10018 or info@skyhorsepublishing.com.

Skyhorse® and Skyhorse Publishing® are registered trademarks of Skyhorse Publishing, Inc.®, a Delaware corporation.

Visit our website at www.skyhorsepublishing.com.

10 9 8 7 6 5 4 3 2 1

Library of Congress Cataloging-in-Publication Data is available on file.

ISBN: 978-1-62636-569-8

Printed in the United States of America

Acquisitions Editor: Jessica Allan
Associate Editor: Allison Scott
Editorial Assistant: Lisa Whitney
Production Editor: Cassandra Margaret Seibel
Copy Editor: Sarah J. Duffy
Typesetter: C&M Digitals (P) Ltd.
Proofreader: Rae-Ann Goodwin
Indexer: Jean Casalegno
Cover Designer: Rose Storey
Permissions Editor: Karen Ehrmann

Contents

Foreword

By definition, children and youth with autism spectrum disorders (ASD) have significant social, communication, and behavioral problems. These challenging learners also frequently experience difficulty in controlling their anger and other emotions. To be sure, educators and parents all too often find themselves in situations where students with autism-related disabilities display meltdown behavior. These problematic and demanding behavioral crises require that supervising adults both engage in appropriate preventative planning and apply evidence-based procedures and tactics.

Without a doubt there is a significant need for evidence-based, practical, and practitioner-friendly resources that help practitioners and families plan for, circumvent, mitigate, and respond to meltdown behavior problems. *Managing the Cycle of Meltdowns for Students With Autism Spectrum Disorder* is a significant source of such information. Colvin and Sheehan's meltdown cycle model reflects years of educational and clinical experience with children and youth with special needs and disabilities, including those with ASD. The strategies they recommend for responding to and managing individuals in various phases of the meltdown cycle are scientifically supported and clearly described. The knowledge and skills that are advanced in *Managing the Cycle of Meltdowns for Students With Autism Spectrum Disorder* are significant, and teachers, related service educational professionals such as speech pathologists and occupational therapists, teaching assistants, and others who work directly with students with autism-related disabilities will find this book to be a valuable resource. Parents and family members will also find the information to be a valuable source of guidance relative to dealing with difficult situations and mitigating problems connected to behavioral crises and urgent problems.

The ASD field is undeniably in its infancy relative to identifying and using the most effective and utilitarian methods for children and youth with ASD. Fortunately, some promising signs on this front can be seen, including efforts by professional associations and individuals to vet the myriad interventions and treatments for children and youth with ASD that purport to improve functioning and quality of life for these learners and their families. These efforts portend favorably for wide-scale adoption of a "best practice" model that is underpinned by procedures, strategies, and other methods with the greatest potential for benefitting learners with ASD and a willingness on the part of stakeholders to consistently use with fidelity maximally effective methods as the foundation for their educational programs.

While general progress on this front is evident, it is also obvious that a number of specific topics relative to effectively serving students with ASD are long overdue for attention. One such neglected area is improving our understanding of behavioral meltdowns among children and youth with ASD and dissemination of utilitarian strategies for preventing and responding to these all-too-common events. In this connection, Colvin and Sheehan have significantly advanced our understanding of meltdown behavior. They offer practitioners and parents proactive recommendations for understanding not only factors associated with meltdown and crisis behaviors but also how to deal with these significant problems. In sum, *Managing the Cycle of Meltdowns for Students with Autism Spectrum Disorder* reflects a sophisticated and multifaceted understanding of a particularly challenging and poorly understood problem of children and youth with ASD. Most important, the practical and practitioner-friendly behavior management and behavior support strategies advanced in this resource bode well for students with ASD being able to learn alternatives to meltdown behavior and ultimately acquire self-control skills that are needed for positive educational and life outcomes.

Richard L. Simpson
Professor of Special Education
University of Kansas, Lawrence, KS

Acknowledgments

We are very grateful to the many professionals who met with us and shared their expertise drawn from extensive experience in the field of autism spectrum disorders and for their valuable feedback on aspects of our manuscript: Janet Conklin, Jennifer DeMott, Deb Egan, Robin Hartshorne, Stacy Howard, and Donna Libby from Lane Education Service District, Eugene, Oregon; and MaryAnne Gates and Mindy LeRoux from Bethel School District, Eugene, Oregon. Thanks are also due to Maggie Hegarty, in Melbourne, Australia, for sharing her written reflections on children with autism.

Several teachers and school personnel are to be thanked for making it possible for us to visit classrooms and directly observe current instructional and management practices in classrooms and schools: Lynne Bronson, Kim Condon, Jennifer DeMott, Wendy Kenyon, and Barbara Willoughby from Lane School, Eugene, Oregon, and Springfield School District, Oregon.

We sincerely acknowledge Kylee Lee for her excellent graphic design contributions in generating the graphs used throughout the manuscript.

Publisher's Acknowledgments

We are grateful for the contributions of the following reviewers:

Carole S. Campbell
Early Childhood Consultant
First Focus on Kids
Tucson, AZ

Wendy Dallman
Special Education Teacher, retired
Substitute Teacher and Facilitator, New Teacher Mentoring Program
School District of New London
Member, Board of Directors, and Counselor, Camp AweSum (camp
    for children and families on the autism spectrum)
New London, WI

Mandy Ellis
Special Education Teacher and Learning Intervention Specialist
Dunlap School District #323
Peoria, IL

Shannan McNair, EdD
Associate Professor
Human Development and Child Studies
Oakland University
Rochester, MI

About the Authors

 **Dr. Geoff Colvin** draws on his experience as a classroom teacher in both special and general education, school administrator, behavior consultant, and research associate at the University of Oregon. He is a nationally recognized educational consultant who has assisted personnel in more than 200 school districts and agencies, nationally and internationally, on the subject of managing problem behavior, teaching and managing students with serious problem behavior and learning challenges, and school safety planning. He has authored and coauthored more than 80 publications, including two current best sellers with Corwin, *7 Steps for Developing a Proactive Schoolwide Discipline Plan* and *Defusing Disruptive Behavior in the Classroom,* and the 2000 Telly Award–winning video program *Defusing Anger and Aggression.*

As an administrator, he directed a juvenile detention school for 5 years and was the principal of a countywide school for seriously emotionally disturbed youth for 5 years. He served as the supervisor of special programs with Bethel School District, in Eugene, Oregon, for several years, where he still serves as a consultant.

Dr. Colvin has a very special skill in being able to translate theory into practice. He is able to present clear explanations and analyses of learning and behavior and at the same time offer concrete examples with hands-on illustrations. His extensive knowledge and experience base, lively speaking style, and keen sense of humor have made him a highly sought-after speaker at national and international conferences.

Presently, he serves as a national educational and behavioral consultant and textbook author.

Dr. Martin R. Sheehan integrates a background in research psychology, direct instruction, special education, and media development. He is the owner of Double S Instructional Systems and has received federal funding for more than 10 National Institutes of Health (NIH) Small Business grant projects. He has served as the principal investigator for projects on improving anger management for adults with disabilities, positive behavior supports for educators who work with challenging students, dangerous drug prevention, nutrition, weight loss and exercise, leisure, and future planning programs for individuals with developmental disabilities.

For 12 years he worked as an administrator in charge of programs for high school students with moderate to severe developmental disabilities. At that time he developed and supervised classrooms for students with autism and other developmental disabilities who exhibited severe acting-out behaviors.

Dr. Sheehan also has worked as a therapist for a local counseling center and specialized in helping individuals with autism and other developmental disabilities as well as helping parents with their difficult children.

He continues to serve on numerous NIH Center for Scientific Review study groups, including the Biobehavioral and Social Science Review Group in the area of Risk, Prevention, and Health Behavior.

Introduction

There is no question that students with autism spectrum disorder (ASD) pose significant challenges to educators, parents, support professionals, and community service providers. These children have profound and quite elusive problems arising from their unique and diverse needs, such as serious limitations with social interactions, verbal and nonverbal communication issues, engagement in repetitive and stereotyped movements, resistance to any changes in their environment, and atypical responses to sensory experiences. These children show considerable variability in intellectual abilities and may or may not be capable of performing at the level needed to be successful in school and graduate with a high school diploma. These factors, taken separately or in concert, make for complex demands on teachers, parents, and service providers. The technology for teaching and managing these children needs to be incredibly precise for adequate learning to take place.

While there are significant challenges for teaching and managing students with ASD—as there are in working with children with any disability for that matter—there is one additional layer of critical concern. Children with ASD often display what is commonly described as *meltdown behavior*. This general class of serious problem behavior manifests itself in many different ways such as sustained screaming and yelling, running away, physical aggression, destruction of property, self-abuse, defiance and noncompliance, throwing things, tantrums, severe withdrawal, and many forms of angry and frustrated outbursts, rage, and acting-out behavior. These meltdowns can occur in classrooms and any other school setting, at home, and anywhere in public. The behaviors appear to have no limits with intensity, frequency, or duration and can occur with any person or persons and in any setting. As expected, these meltdowns can take an incredible toll on teachers, parents and their families, professional service providers, and the individual persons with ASD.

Moreover, teachers and parents have often reported that they have dealt with other children before who display tantrums and serious acting-out behavior. In these cases they can usually determine what sets off the problems in the first place, can make appropriate adjustments, have a sense of where the child is coming from, and can work through these problem behaviors satisfactorily for the most part. However, this is usually not the case when dealing with meltdowns from children with ASD. Even though the behaviors may look like tantrums and acting-out behavior, they are not. Teachers and parents often have difficulty knowing when the outbursts may occur and often their standard interventions for tantrums and acting-out behavior not only are ineffective but often exacerbate the situations.

This book addresses the unique characteristics and needs of children with ASD with a primary focus on meltdowns. We describe procedures for analyzing meltdown behavior and developing strategies for effective interventions to be used by educators, parents, and service providers.

The book is divided into two sections. The purpose of the first section is to provide background and details on the development of a model for understanding the meltdown cycle for students with ASD. Chapter 1 presents an overview of the distinctive characteristics of students with ASD. It is assumed that a deeper understanding of their unique needs will lead to more accurate and appropriate assessment and intervention plans for addressing meltdown behavior. Chapter 2 discusses the nature of meltdowns. Chapter 3 presents information on the development and detail of a conceptual model for meltdown behavior. An analysis of a meltdown behavioral cycle is presented, followed by a description of a model comprising six clearly defined phases, each of which depicts characteristic behaviors of children with ASD during a meltdown cycle. Common behavioral features are delineated for each phase in the model that allows staff to develop a specific behavior profile for a student with ASD who displays meltdown behavior. Once this profile has been determined, staff are in a strong position to develop a comprehensive behavior support plan to manage all phases of the meltdown cycle.

The second section, Chapters 4–10, which constitutes the bulk of the book, is devoted to an explanation and description of many strategies for managing each of the six phases in the meltdown cycle. The strategies selected are taken from research and best practice procedures reported in the literature and practiced in the field. Since each phase represents a link in the behavioral cycle, effective management of the early phases is emphasized to preempt the later, more serious behavior of meltdowns from occurring. The goal is to *disrupt* the meltdown cycle, thereby preventing a behavioral meltdown. Emphasis in this book is placed on teaching and prevention techniques in the early phases of the cycle. In the later phases, the approach stresses safety, crisis management, reentry, and follow-up procedures. The overall approach is to develop a behavior support plan consisting of strategies to address each phase in the meltdown cycle. Chapters 4–9 describe details of the plan for implementation in the classroom and school. The final chapter, Chapter 10, addresses the critical role of parents in developing a behavior support plan and details for the specific component to be implemented by parents at home and in the community.

The reader is referred to an Appendices section at the back of the book that contains all of the forms presented throughout the book. These forms may be reproduced or adapted for personal use in the classroom or home.

SECTION 1

A Model for Meltdown Behavior of Students with ASD

1

Autism Spectrum Disorder, Overview

O ne of the biggest challenges facing teachers and sources of stress and burnout is the student with behavior problems (R. Ingersoll & Smith, 2003; Oliver & Reschly, 2007). Especially difficult are students who exhibit severe and disruptive acting-out behaviors. A group of students who frequently exhibit acting-out behaviors and who are now placed in general education classrooms, resource rooms, and self-contained classrooms are those with autism spectrum disorder (ASD; Lecavalier, Leone, & Wiltz, 2006).

ASD is a disability characterized by deficits in three major areas—social interaction, communication, and imagination (American Psychiatric Association, 2000). At one end of the spectrum are children with classic autism that is marked by significant deficits in speech and cognition. At the other end of the spectrum are individuals who have normal to superior intelligence, more typical language abilities, but still significant difficulties dealing with social interactions and managing their emotions (Frith, 1991). This group has been referred to as having high-functioning autism or Asperger syndrome. The broad category of ASD is currently being conceptualized as a single spectrum that ranges from most severe ASD to less severe ASD (American Psychiatric Association, 2010). The past decade has seen a significant increase in the number of children identified with ASD, with prevalence estimates ranging from 1 in 110 (Centers for Disease Control and Prevention, 2009) to 1 in 150 (Stevens et al., 2007). This trend is in contrast to several other disabilities whose identified numbers have been decreasing, for example, specific learning disabilities, mental retardation, and emotional disturbances (Scull & Winkler, 2011). A common question raised by school officials is this: What accounts for this increase in ASD? The reasons are generally considered to be unclear as to whether there has been an increase because other factors are also present. The clinical definition of autism now includes a wider spectrum of behaviors. Parents, teachers, and other professionals are generally more aware of autism. Some of the children previously diagnosed as having an intellectual disability are now receiving a primary diagnosis of autism. Moreover, more services are available for children identified with ASD. All of these factors may play an important role in the increase in the number of individuals now being identified with ASD (Stein, 2007).

The term *autism* is frequently considered to refer to a medical condition involving neurological abnormalities, the actual causes of which are still being investigated in medical research. It is expected that this research will continue and provide more direction in terms of how students with autism can be better served in society. In addition, it is widely held that genetic factors contribute to the disability as well. However, for the purposes of this book, we focus on educational issues, specifically on how the disability of autism affects the student's learning and behavior in school. In particular the focus is on what individuals with ASD actually *do*—responses made in the classroom, performance levels on tasks, and activities in which the students become engaged, learn, and behave appropriately. It is understood that everything a student does is linked to many interacting factors—perceptions, motor capabilities, cognitions, language, social interactions, and emotions (Thelen, 2008; Thelen & Smith, 1996). Even the simplest behavior is a combination of many factors, each of which must be considered in efforts to understand ASD and to provide educational services for students with this disability (Novak & Pelaez, 2011; Pelaez-Nogueras, 1996).

What follows is a description of seven major characteristic patterns of behavior commonly exhibited by students with ASD: (1) deficits in social interactions; (2) deficits in verbal and nonverbal communication; (3) restricted, repetitive patterns of behavior, interests, and activities; (4) atypical responses to sensory experiences; (5) deficits in cognitive abilities; (6) physical and emotional health; and (7) motor skill difficulties.

Deficits in Social Interactions

The most striking feature of people with ASD is the problem they have with social interactions (Attwood, 2007; Volkmar & Weisner, 2009). Some individuals are totally disconnected from other people, often treating them like objects, such as a piece of furniture. Others are passive in how they accept social overtures from others, and they rarely, if ever, initiate interactions. Some students with ASD have social behaviors that center on their obsessions, such as their need to talk about their fixed interests, and their overall resistance to sharing. Other interpersonal difficulties include insensitivity to the feelings of others and a failure to understand why people act the way they do. Students with ASD may rigidly apply codes of conduct and rules without really understanding them.

These underlying difficulties in social interactions may lead to problems when contacting other people, understanding other people, and making sense of rules in a given social situation. For example, in classrooms teachers use rules and routines frequently and a student may not follow the rule because he or she does not understand it or thinks that it applies only to a given situation. Consequently, the teacher corrects the student or provides a prompt that can cause the student to resist and exhibit problem behavior. Moreover, the unusual behaviors and lack of social skills often lead to the student being teased and bullied, resulting in stress, frustration, and eventually a meltdown.

Deficits in Verbal and Nonverbal Communication

There is a wide range of communication skills and deficits in students with ASD (Attwood, 2007; Tager-Flusberg, Paul, & Lord, 2005). Some students with the most severe forms of autism never develop speech, only learn to echo others' words, or have significant speech delays. Many students with ASD have difficulties in the use of social language, especially in conversations. They often engage in one-sided unending monologues about their topic of interest. They have difficulty expressing their needs. They also have problems with the nonverbal aspects of communication, using inappropriate body language, not making eye contact, and misinterpreting other people's body language, facial expressions, and tone of voice.

Students with ASD who have difficulty conveying their thoughts and feelings may become frustrated and angry, and exhibit disruptive behaviors. Students with little or no speech may use aggression and tantrums as a means of communication or as a result of frustration from not being understood. The problems with communication that students with ASD experience contribute to many of the acting-out behaviors that they show, which can, in turn, lead to meltdowns.

Restricted, Repetitive Patterns of Behavior, Interests, and Activities

Self-stimulatory behavior is often seen in young students with ASD or students with very severe ASD, such as flapping their hands, rocking, spinning objects, flicking their fingers, banging their heads, or grinding their teeth (Bodfish, Symons, Parker, & Lewis, 2000; Turner, 1999). There are several possible explanations for these behaviors. They may simply be enjoyable for the students. Simple repetitive actions are their way of dealing with stress, anxiety, physical illness, pain, or overwhelming sensory input. Self-stimulatory behaviors could also be used to get attention from teachers or to escape from an unpleasant task. In its extreme form, self-stimulatory behaviors can become self-injurious to indicate that the students are very upset. These behaviors include hand biting, intense scratching, face slapping, and head banging.

Students with ASD demand structure and predictability in their lives (Attwood, 2007; Szatmari et al., 2006). They have great difficulty handling transitions and change. They may develop elaborate rituals whereby things have to be done in a certain way and no deviation can be tolerated. Changes in the school schedule, such as assemblies, interrupt their rituals and can lead to meltdowns. This need for sameness can also affect their social interactions with other students. They may insist on playing by certain rules and may try to enforce their rules on others. When peers do not comply with their wishes, students with ASD may become extremely upset and tantrum.

These students tend to have very narrow interests and become obsessed with special topics (Abramson et al., 2005). They may have a large collection of facts and figures on a specific topic such as trains, spiders, and so on. This can lead to difficulties concentrating on things like schoolwork. This obsessive quality of their special interests presents challenges for the teacher who tries to get such a student to focus on the task at hand while the student is only interested in his or her topic of fascination. Attempts to get the student to focus frequently leads to acting-out behaviors.

Atypical Responses to Sensory Experiences

Many students with ASD are oversensitive to sensory experiences compared to students without disabilities (Bogdashina, 2003; Rogers & Ozonoff, 2005). They may be oversensitive to sound, light, taste, smell, and touch. Other students with ASD may be undersensitive, for example, not hearing the teacher when spoken to (even though their hearing is not a problem). Some areas may be especially troublesome, like noisy corridors, locker areas, or lunchrooms. The classroom itself may be too bright, be too crowded, have too many distractions on the walls, and be too noisy.

The flicker of the fluorescent lights can be especially difficult to handle for students with ASD. Many students on the spectrum do not like being touched. They have a difficult time when other students, or the teacher, encroach on their personal space. Fire alarms, bells, and sirens can all cause stressful reactions. Strong odors emanating from the cafeteria, certain perfumes, and aftershave lotions can cause negative reactions. Any of these sensory factors singly, jointly, or in combination with other areas of difficulty can serve as triggers that can lead to serious problem behaviors.

Deficits in Cognitive Abilities

There are several impaired cognitive abilities for individuals with ASD (Minshew & Goldstein, 1998; D. L. Williams, Goldstein, & Minshew, 2006). These students frequently have difficulty focusing on relevant information and trouble tuning out distractions. While their rote memory is adequate, they tend to overly rely on it and miss the main point of what is being studied. Other learning difficulties include problems with organization, problem solving, and concept formation. Students with ASD can handle only small amounts of new information, have problems remembering complex material, and become preoccupied with details and parts of objects. It takes them more time to process new material. And they tend to literally interpret metaphors and misunderstand jokes, humor, and sarcasm (D. L. Williams & Minshew, 2010).

Learning difficulties can have a strong impact on how well they are able to cope with academic demands. Schoolwork can become very difficult, leaving students with ASD feeling upset and frustrated, which can lead to them exhibiting challenging behaviors.

Physical and Emotional Health

Many students with ASD have sleep problems (Malow et al., 2006; G. P. Williams, Sears, & Allard, 2004). They may have trouble going to sleep, staying asleep, waking up early, and getting enough sleep. Many parents report that their children with ASD have stomach problems (Buie et al., 2010). Chief among these complaints are constipation, stomachaches, and diarrhea. There may also be problems with eating. Children with ASD are frequently very picky eaters and often only eat and drink specific foods and beverages.

A high frequency of mood and anxiety disorders has been reported for this population (Matson & Nebel-Schwalm, 2007; White, Oswald, Ollendick, & Scahill, 2009). Students with ASD may have great difficulty in managing their stress and have problems with self-esteem and depression. Negative reactions frequently occur when a person with ASD is hungry, feeling ill, tired, frustrated, or emotionally stressed.

Motor Skill Difficulties

Despite the fact that early views on motor development emphasized that students with ASD had normal or even advanced motor development, recent research has reported that they frequently appear clumsy, have motor coordination abnormalities, exhibit postural instability, and perform poorly on tests of motor functioning (Fournier, Hass, Naik, Lodha, & Cauraugh, 2010; Ming, Brimacombe, & Wagner, 2007; Ozonoff et al., 2008). Motor deficits can make life very difficult and frustrating for these students. They face challenges in mastering basic life skills such as dressing, teeth brushing, and toileting; participating in physical education classes, sports involving hand-eye coordination, or recess activities, such as bike riding and playing games; and participating in class instruction involving problems with fine motor skills in handwriting, coloring, and manipulating materials in certain class projects.

Chapter Summary

For many years, the subject of autism has undergone ongoing research at both medical and educational levels. One result has been an increasing awareness of this disability among professionals and parents, giving rise to increased identification in the community and in public schools. Moreover, the definition of the disability has been substantially broadened from simply autism to *autism spectrum disorders*. This term reflects the wide range of handicapping conditions associated with this broader identification category.

Students with ASD present a unique set of challenges in terms of both providing effective instruction and learning opportunities and managing behavior (especially when it comes to serious acting-out behavior). These students have deficits in many areas that significantly impact their learning and behavior—substantial social thinking deficits, communication difficulties, rigid behaviors and inflexible thinking, sensory sensitivities, health-related issues, motor skill limitations, and learning difficulties. These characteristics singly and in combination greatly increase the probability of students' acting-out behaviors leading to meltdowns at school, at home, and in the community. Under the constant strain of having to deal with a world that is frequently confusing and intrusive, students with ASD may feel stressed, become frustrated, and lose control, resulting in tantrums and meltdowns. Educators and parents must make ongoing efforts to better understand the critical role these unique characteristics play in the lives of these students. In this way, the necessary support may be provided for students to learn, behave appropriately, and grow up to enjoy a reasonably happy and fruitful life.

2

The Nature of Meltdowns

A highly charged word that typically brings much dismay to parents, educators, and service providers of children with autism spectrum disorder (ASD) is *meltdowns*. In general, meltdowns refer to the extreme actions exhibited by children with ASD when they reach an intense state of out-of-control behavior, such as screaming, tantrums, destruction of property, thrashing on the floor, running away, physical tension, and physical attacks on self and others. These outbursts can pose serious safety concerns and can substantially disrupt the environment where the meltdown occurs, whether it is the classroom, other school settings, home, or the community. Supervising adults are usually unable to interrupt the meltdown, so these explosive behaviors will run their course. The usual recourse is to make the situation as safe as possible for the child, other children, and the adults themselves. The long-term impact can be devastating. Parents often report that the threat of meltdowns significantly curtails their lifestyle by limiting their outings in the community, having visitors to their home, visiting the homes of friends and relatives, travel, holidays, and using childcare (sitters) at home. Similarly, teachers indicate that they have to be very selective with school activities that they make available to students with ASD who are prone to meltdowns. Clearly, there is a grave need to more fully address meltdown behavior of students with ASD so that more refined tools can be developed for preventing, interrupting, and managing this severe and very challenging behavior.

The purpose of this chapter is to closely examine the nature of meltdowns exhibited by students with ASD, which Thompson (2009) aptly refers to as the *anatomy of a meltdown*. The approach in understanding meltdowns is to carefully analyze two instances of situations that lead to them. These examples then set the stage for identifying contributing factors and tracking the corresponding responses from the child during the meltdown event. This review leads to a working definition for meltdowns and, most important, provide the basis for the development of a model for describing the meltdown cycle (described in Chapter 3).

This chapter investigates the following: (1) two examples of meltdown behavior, (2) preliminary observations, (3) detailed analyses, (4) working definition of a meltdown, and (5) the need for a new model.

Two Examples of Meltdown Behavior

In the following examples, students in a typical classroom exhibit a range of behaviors leading up to, during, and following a meltdown. The setting and interactions with the teacher and other events are described in Box 2.1.

| Box 2.1 | Examples of Meltdown Behavior for Students With ASD |

Elementary Student

Background

Ricky is a 5-year-old boy with autism. He never initiates conversations and rarely makes eye contact with other individuals. He has difficulty communicating with his peers and usually does not respond when people speak to him. On a regular basis, Ricky becomes upset and has serious meltdowns involving screaming, throwing things around, rushing around the room, and flailing his arms.

His parents report that his behavior at school and at home has worsened in that he is having more meltdowns since they moved to a different area of town and a new school. Presently, he is placed in a special education

(Continued)

(Continued)

class at the local elementary school. His teacher reports that she has been unable to find effective teaching strategies to work with Ricky. She says that he is very disruptive in class when he has his meltdowns and that she has to remove the rest of the class to an adjacent room so teaching can continue and he can then calm down. At this stage she has been unable to identify the triggers, and when he does escalate it goes very fast.

Meltdown Incident

The students were milling around the front of the class near the teacher at the beginning of class. The front of the room was quite noisy and crowded. The teacher assistant approached Ricky as she worked one on one with him for language. Ricky jumped up and ran to the corner of the room and started screaming. He sat on the floor, put his hands over his ears, and continued to scream, thrashing his legs. The teacher assistant sat beside him and then Ricky ran off to another area of the room, continuing to scream. The teacher has a practice of a "room clear" when Ricky goes off like this. So the teacher and another assistant took the rest of the students to an adjacent small room, leaving Ricky and the teacher assistant in the classroom with the connecting door open. Ricky continued to scream and flail his arms, with the teacher assistant standing some distance from him. After about 5 minutes the screaming subsided and Ricky sat on the floor with his hands over his ears. The teacher assistant waited a few more minutes and sat on a nearby chair. The teacher assistant put some Legos on the floor and began building a house, putting some Legos near Ricky. She then prompted Ricky to help with building the house and handed him some Legos. He took the items and began to assemble them. The other students, the teacher, and the other assistant reentered the classroom and continued with their spelling groups.

The teacher commented that she does not feel she is teaching Ricky very much and that most of the time is spent just trying to engage him and to minimize the meltdowns.

Secondary Student

Background

Elena is a 15-year-old girl with Asperger syndrome. She does best when teachers and staff respond to her interests. She likes to talk about her hobbies, such as her card collection of pop singers, and talks with more animation when staff show interest by responding to her comments. She can stay focused for lengthy periods, especially with tasks that are routine and have definite closure, as in completing a page of writing or math. She enjoys independent activities such as computer games and watching TV or video programs and games.

Elena has little interest in socializing with students her own age. She tends to talk about her area of interest (TV stars, especially female singers) and does not pay any attention to what the other person might be talking about. Her speech is overly formal and pedantic, and she loves to relay factual information about her favorite singers and the songs they sing and when you can watch them on TV. She loves playing computer games and spends all of her free time doing this or watching her stars on TV. She dislikes playing sports and refuses to take part in PE class. She has a large collection of pencils and never goes anywhere without at least one pencil.

Meltdown Incident

Elena was at her desk looking at cards of her favorite singers while the teacher was explaining something to the class. The teacher directed Elena to put her cards away as it was time for class and she could sort them later during break. Elena said to wait one minute. She put her head down and started moving the cards quickly and mumbled to herself. The teacher moved toward her, knowing that she would play with the cards all day if permitted. The teacher said quite firmly that the cards needed to be put away right now and pushed one of the cards toward the center of her desk. Elena reacted quite strongly by shouting, "Leave my cards alone." The teacher told her to leave her cards and that she needed to go to the time-out area and quiet down. Elena grabbed her cards and kicked the chair over on her way to the time-out area, shouting that the cards were hers. The teacher followed her. In the time-out area, Elena began to pound on the walls, rip up materials, and kick the desk, screaming that the cards are hers. The teacher withdrew, watching her from a short distance. Elena eventually sat down, gathered her cards, and held them. She then sat in the corner, still very upset, and began to sort her cards. When she was finished she folded her arms and stared at the floor for some time. The teacher approached her and gave her a form to complete, which she did but quite slowly. When Elena had completed the form, she was directed to join the class, which she did. Toward the end of the period, when Elena was engaged with the class, the teacher reviewed the form with her and addressed how she could have sorted her cards without the big scene. Elena mumbled a lot during the meeting but cooperated overall.

Preliminary Observations

There are several similarities in these two examples:

1. Each teacher gave a direction to the student. Ricky was asked to get ready for spelling (language), and Elena was directed to put her cards away and attend to the class instructions.

2. The students continued with what they were doing.

3. The teachers persisted with their directions.

4. The students escalated further. Ricky rushed to the corner of the room screaming and fell down on the floor. Elena grabbed her cards and shouted at the teacher.

5. Each teacher approached his or her student, resulting in further escalation of meltdown behavior, involving serious disruptive behavior.

6. Each student ended up removed from the instructional setting. Ricky ran to another part of the room, and the class moved to an adjacent room. Elena was in the time-out area.

At first glance, the teachers' responses to the situations involving Ricky and Elena appear to be reasonable and consistent with standard classroom practices. Both students were prompted to begin the scheduled class activity. However, in each case, the situation worsened, with both students resisting their teacher's directions. Moreover, each student showed an escalation in behavior to the extent that they were removed from the instructional area and a meltdown involving serious disruptive behavior occurred.

Some important questions arise. What is likely to happen in the future? Can we expect more of these serious outbursts? Could they escalate even further, involving physical harm to the students having the meltdown, teachers, or other students? What could have been done differently to manage these situations so that the problems could have been avoided in the first place or at least defused once they were evident? Answers to these questions begin with a detailed analyses designed to identify factors that may have contributed to the meltdown situations.

Detailed Analyses

It is clear, at the outset, that the contributing factors to each of the meltdowns in the illustrations were a combination of, or an interaction between, events in the classroom environment and factors arising from the disability of ASD. In these two illustrations, several of these interacting variables need to be considered in order to better understand meltdowns and to more effectively manage these and similar incidents: (a) the classroom set-up; (b) teacher–student interactions; (c) the role of triggers, ASD characteristics, and agitation; (d) functions of the behavior; (e) escalating behavior chains; (f) follow-up; and (g) the meltdown cycle.

The Classroom Set-Up

For both Ricky and Elena, classroom procedures contributed significantly to their meltdowns. The students milling around the teacher at the front of the class, with accompanying noise and crowding, probably triggered Ricky's agitation, as he is very sensitive to noise (although the triggers for him are quite varied). Similarly, Elena was already playing with her cards after the lesson was underway. Elena is possessive of her cards and has strong compulsions to complete her routines once she is underway.

Teacher–Student Interactions

Teachers typically follow through when they present directions to students, given the expectation that students cooperate with teacher directions. When students do not follow the directions, teachers usually use procedures such as acknowledging cooperative students, repeating the direction or approaching the students, and providing more focus on the direction. However, when the teacher does follow through, some students react to the additional steps taken that involve further interactions with the teacher. Both Ricky and Elena reacted negatively to their teachers' attempts to follow through with directions, resulting in additional interactions with their teacher (when the teacher assistant approached Ricky and when Elena was asked to put her cards away).

It was evident in each of these situations that interactions occurred involving both teacher and student behavior once the teacher tried to prompt the student to engage in the required tasks. For each teacher behavior there was a corresponding student behavior and vice versa. In the case of Ricky, the teacher assistant approaching him and then following him and sitting beside him appeared to escalate the situation or maintain the escalation once Ricky started screaming. In the case of Elena, the successive teacher–student interactions played a key role in the escalation process. Each successive student behavior was preceded by a specific teacher behavior. Or it could be argued that each teacher behavior was preceded by a specific student behavior. In this sense, the teacher behavior may have set the stage for the next student behavior and the student behavior may have set the stage for the next teacher behavior.

The Role of Triggers, ASD Characteristics, and Agitation

It is very common for students with ASD to become agitated when certain triggers are present. In Ricky's case the excessive noise and crowding at the front of the class, the teacher assistant approaching him, or both served as triggers for him as he is very sensitive to noise levels and crowded settings (a sensory stimulation characteristic). Similarly, when the teacher moved one of Elena's cards, she became upset and started shouting. She does not like to have her routines disrupted or have others interfere with her prize collection. Her trigger was an interrupted routine set up by the characteristic of the need for sameness and predictability.

Note: We are not suggesting that teachers should not intervene or deliver directions—rather it is important to understand how the interventions can impact student behavior. We are trying to establish that certain approaches under specific conditions are likely to trigger more problem behavior. The implication is that we need to use different approaches that show cognizance of factors that escalate behavior and adjust our approaches accordingly.

Functions of the Behavior

Both Ricky and Elena had a way of trying to control the problems they faced. Ricky wanted to control the noise and crowding, so he began to scream and run around the room. He was successful in getting away from the disturbing noise by having the class go to another room, and he was left by himself with a teacher assistant. Similarly, Elena wanted to preserve the sameness and predictability when she was sorting her cards. Her teacher wanted her to stop sorting her cards and join the class. By acting out and refusing to cooperate with the teacher, she was sent to the time-out area. In this way she was successful in being able to continue sorting her cards.

Escalating Behavior Chains

Once the teachers approached and interacted further with Ricky and Elena, each student became more agitated and displayed more intense behavior. The students' verbal responses became louder, physical gestures or actions became more vigorous, and both students left their instructional settings (Ricky ran to the corner and Elena went to the time-out area). This whole process can be described as an escalating behavior chain, in which each ensuing behavior is more serious than the one preceding it, leading to the last one, the most disruptive of all—a meltdown. In Ricky's case, the escalation was much quicker. It is very important to note that each response from the students was preceded by a response from the teacher. In effect, the teachers' responses to the students served as cues for the successive student responses in the escalating behavior chains. Moreover, in the case of students with ASD, the escalation of acting-out behavior can occur very quickly. This implies that problem behavior needs to be addressed very early in the chain.

Follow-Up

The teachers left the two students alone but kept an eye on them. Each student quieted down. Since Ricky's communication skills are so low, any form of debriefing or direct follow-up with him would not be productive. However, the teacher and assistant met later to review what had happened, what may have triggered the melt-down, and what adjustments they would make in the future. In Elena's case, later on, after the students were underway in class, the teacher met with her and conducted a debriefing session with guided problem-solving activity and encouragement to do better next time.

It is quite evident, through this preliminary analysis of the factors contributing to the meltdown incidents, that the situations could have been managed more effectively. The implication is that teachers need to carefully examine environmental factors in the classroom that may escalate students' acting-out behavior and, at the same time, have an understanding of the children's needs and where they are coming from in order to manage their behavior more effectively.

The Meltdown Cycle

A crucial question to be asked in each of these cases is whether the same problem behaviors will occur again. If things remain much the same, the answer would be a decided yes. If the same triggers are present (noise level and crowding for Ricky and interruption of card routine or other established routines with Elena), the students would become agitated. If similar teacher–student interactions occur again, the students would escalate. Moreover, in each case the student ended up being left alone, which presumably is what they wanted—escape from the situation. If the last behavior, or behavior toward the end of the chain, is strongly reinforced, then it is highly likely that the whole chain will be reinforced, which was the case for each of these students (they were left alone). So yes, these meltdown behaviors for each student would most likely be repeated. That is, a meltdown cycle of acting-out behavior would be established and, as such, become quite challenging to address effectively.

Working Definition of a Meltdown

The question now arises: What exactly is a meltdown? The term *meltdown* has been used in common language, or everyday English, to mean an internal collapse. For example, a nuclear meltdown refers to a major defect in the cooling system causing extensive over-heating, resulting in melting of the radioactive core and escape of life-threatening radiation. The term is also used to convey collapses in other areas, such as the recent disastrous effects in the financial world when there was a subprime meltdown. Interests rates were significantly lowered, enabling a proliferation of loans to people with poor credit, so when the interest rates rose many homeowners defaulted in loan payments, resulting in huge numbers of foreclo-sures and bankruptcies for homeowners and lending institutions. The term *meltdown* is also used in everyday language to communicate that people, through cumulative stress and problems, reach a point when they snap, become very angry, and go berserk—they have an emo-tional meltdown. Temple Grandin used the term "catastrophic reac-tions" in referring to the more intense and sustained meltdowns (Lipsky & Richards, 2009, p. 24).

The term *meltdown* has also become a key concept in the field of ASD. Two approaches are taken to provide a working or operational definition: distinction between meltdowns and tantrums, and critical features of a meltdown.

Distinction Between Meltdowns and Tantrums

Educators and parents are usually quite familiar with tantrums in children. These behaviors have often been called *acting-out behav-ior, temper outbursts, out-of-control behavior,* and *emotional flare-ups.* The behaviors have high levels of intensity, seriously disrupt the environment, and can pose safety hazards to the individual and others in close proximity. In many cases, tantrums are considered to be developmental. That is, the behaviors are something that all or most children display in the early stages of their childhood, with reductions in frequency and intensity as the children grow older. Many parents are familiar with the terrible twos, which is the age that tantrums and oppositional behavior are typically the worst during early childhood. Some children, however, may display these behaviors throughout their childhood and into adulthood. Adults can exhibit acting-out behavior in the form of rage, assault, self-abuse, and suicide, and may assume addictive habits such as alcoholism and drug abuse. In effect, tantrums or acting-out behaviors are quite common among children as a part of growing up and are, unfortunately, a concern that is relatively common among adults. In these cases, the individual exhibits tantrums as a child and carries the behavior into adulthood. One apt description for this developmental progression from tantrums in childhood to adulthood is that these children do not grow out of tantrums; they grow into them.

In the case of children with ASD, the term *meltdown* is commonly used to describe outbursts and sustained acting-out behavior. On the surface, one might wonder why a separate term is used. Teachers and parents typically report that the behaviors look the same—a child with ASD in a *meltdown* exhibits the same intensive behaviors as another child, without disabilities, who is throwing a serious *tantrum*. The reason a separate term is used in the field is that there are several underlying differences that have important implications for interventions and service.

It is clear the behaviors displayed by a student with ASD in a meltdown have the same appearances as another student who is exhibiting a severe tantrum. In each case the behaviors have high intensity, disrupt the environment, and pose safety concerns. However, the behaviors can be seen to be very different when a more detailed analysis is conducted. These differences are listed in Table 2.1. Elaborations on differences are presented in Chapter 3 and Section II.

Note: These differences are to be seen as general descriptors only. In practice there will most likely be overlap between these two divisions in that some characteristics will be shared with some students. Moreover, the fact that the word *spectrum* is used in ASD indicates that a full range of behavioral variation across individual students is to be expected. However, this division may help educators and parents understand the nuances of differences between meltdowns and regular tantrums that have implications for effective interventions.

Table 2.1   Differences Between Meltdowns and Tantrums

Features of Meltdowns (For Students With ASD)	Features of Tantrums (Normal Development)
Awareness: The child is not aware or does not seem to care if others are watching or responding.	*Awareness:* The child is aware and looks around to see if others are watching or attending.
Safety: The child usually is unmindful if self or others may be hurt.	*Safety:* The child is usually aware enough not to hurt self.
Developmental Course: Meltdowns may become less frequent as the child grows older or may be life-long unless they are carefully managed.	*Developmental Course:* Behaviors are usually developmental and students "outgrow" them.
Social Impact: The child is usually inattentive to the reaction of others.	*Social Impact:* The child is usually quite aware of impact on others and often uses this to his or her ends.
Runs Course: The meltdown winds down slowly and cannot be stopped suddenly.	*Runs Course:* The tantrum can be interrupted, especially if student attains need.
Duration: The meltdown can last for extended periods of time, as in hours.	*Duration:* The tantrum can be short-lived. It usually stops when the child achieves the goal or realizes the goal will not be obtained.
Degree of Control: The child appears to be out of control and no one can intervene to change the course of action.	*Degree of Control:* The child appears to be in control and can stop the outburst at any time.
Need: Outbursts occur because of a specific need and will continue even when need is met.	*Need:* Outbursts occur because of a specific need and usually stop once the need is met.
Triggers: Outbursts are usually caused by internal triggers such a sensory overload, social issues, or communication failures.	*Triggers:* Outbursts are caused by external factors such as wanting one's own way, needing a specific thing.
Purpose: Behavior is usually reactive to sensory factors, social issues, or communication issues rather than oppositional.	*Purpose:* Behavior is often oppositional or noncompliant.
Interventions: These should focus on sensory management and communication.	*Interventions:* These should focus on manipulating the environment.
Key Difference: Outbursts are driven by need to reduce anxiety.	*Key Difference:* Outbursts are driven by manipulation of environment.

Source: Adapted from www.autism-causes.com/the-meltdown.html.

Critical Features of a Meltdown

For the purposes of this book, a meltdown for students with ASD is described in terms of a number of related behavioral characteristics:

- A behavioral outburst that has high intensity, disrupts the environment, and is often unsafe.
- It is typically triggered by sensory overload, social problems, or communication issues (see fuller description in Chapter 3).
- The outburst usually follows a buildup of anxiety and should not be perceived as manipulative or oppositional.
- A student exhibiting a meltdown is usually oblivious to other people in the environment.
- Meltdowns typically run their course and usually cannot be disrupted once they begin.

The most important point to be made at this juncture is that, although meltdowns exhibited by students with ASD may have observable similarities to the acting-out behavior and tantrums of students without disabilities, there are many significant differences. These differences need to be understood and accommodated in behavioral analyses and subsequent interventions (these topics will be addressed in Chapter 3 and Section II).

Need for a New Model

It is one thing to advocate that meltdowns for children with ASD need to be understood as different from the regular tantrums exhibited by children without disabilities. However, it is quite a challenge to use standard behavioral principles and practices for managing problem behaviors that have demonstrated effectiveness with other students. Teachers and parents have often made comments such as "I use interventions that have been effective with other students, but in the case of my student with ASD the situation does not get better and often gets worse when meltdowns occur."

What is needed is a more refined model for describing the cycle of meltdown behavior that addresses the unique needs and characteristics of children with ASD and at the same time is based on sound empirically based principles and practices. There is a need in the field for a new model. The purpose of this book is to present such a model and to use it for designing systematic interventions plans in order to prevent and manage meltdowns and to establish appropriate replacement behavior.

Chapter Summary

Two examples of common problem situations for students with ASD were presented in this chapter. Each incident involved an escalation of behavior leading to a meltdown in which the level of intensity of the students' behavior reached serious and unsafe levels. Such situations can be described in terms of an escalating chain of behavior with observable, discrete stages. The rate of escalation varies from student to student. In Ricky's case the escalation went very fast, whereas in Elena's case the escalation was much slower, involving several successive teacher–student interactions. Several factors were identified as key events that may have significantly contributed to escalating the student's behavior. An important implication is that if these factors had been addressed in different ways, these two students' meltdowns may have been prevented. It was evident with each example that if these situations arise in the future, then further meltdowns would most likely occur. These patterns suggest that meltdown behavior can be represented as a cycle of behavior comprising identifiable steps leading to a meltdown that will recur.

On the surface meltdowns have many features in common with tantrums exhibited by children as part of their developmental growth. Children who do not have disabilities will grow out of these problems. This is not the case for students with ASD. Several important differences are noted between meltdowns and tantrums. The conclusion is that an approach that is different from the standard behavioral approaches for managing tantrums needs to be taken to prevent and manage meltdowns. There is a need for a new model.

A specific model representing the meltdown cycle is described in Chapter 3 and applied to the two examples of meltdown behavior presented in this chapter. In the remaining chapters, the model is used as a framework for assessing and developing systematic interventions for disrupting the meltdown cycle and establishing appropriate behavior.

3

A Six-Phase Model of the Meltdown Cycle

The escalated behavior pattern leading to meltdowns for students with autism spectrum disorder (ASD), illustrated by the two students, Ricky and Elena, in Chapter 2 (Box 2.1), can be described in terms of a model comprising phases leading to and following a meltdown incident. This model has been adapted from a cyclical representation developed by Colvin (1999, 2004, 2010) for the explosive and disruptive behavior patterns of students with established problem behavior in general and special education. In this chapter, details of the model as applied to students with ASD are presented in the following sections: (1) background on model development, (2) model for describing the meltdown cycle for students with ASD, (3) behavior support plan, and (4) case studies.

Background on Model Development

The model developed by Colvin for depicting serious acting-out behavior in the classroom has been widely adopted in general and special education (Kauffman, Mostert, Trent, & Hallahan, 1998; Sprague & Golly, 2004; Sprick & Garrison, 2008; Walker, Ramsey, & Gresham, 2003). This model depicts serious acting-out behavior in terms of seven phases—*calm, triggers, agitation, acceleration, peak, de-escalation,* and *recovery* (Colvin, 2004). The process begins with students being relatively calm and engaged in class activities. Triggers come into play that impact the students in a way that causes them to lose their focus and become agitated or upset. If the agitation continues, and the triggers continue to operate, the students may become more disturbed and engage the teacher or other students in aggressive or negative ways. These negative interactions usually escalate further to serious acting-out behavior (peak) that is typically very disruptive and often unsafe. Eventually, the students will begin to settle down and enter the de-escalation phase, characterized by the students appearing lost and confused. After further time and opportunity to settle down, the students assume more control of themselves and can recover sufficiently to reenter the class activity. Behavioral descriptions were provided for each of these phases in the acting-out cycle based on information from a large sample of students covering all ages from kindergarten through high school who exhibited this behavioral pattern.

The most significant adaptation of the acting-out model (Colvin, 2004) in applying it to students with ASD was to combine the agitation and acceleration phases into one phase—Agitation. The reason is that the demarcation between these two is not so obvious for students with ASD. These students typically do not attend to or interact with the environment. The meltdowns are driven primarily by an overreaction to sensory overload and a cognitive breakdown stemming from frustrations with communication. In effect, students with ASD who are having a meltdown are mostly oblivious to the environment. Whereas students who do not have ASD and who seriously act out usually try to directly manipulate the environment by engaging staff or other students with behavior *directed to someone*—defiance, threats, confrontation, verbal abuse, and so on. In effect, they *externalize* their behavior and concerns. On the other hand, students with ASD do not attend to or try to engage others. Their meltdown behavior accelerates through internal factors. They *internalize* their behavior and concerns. Consequently, in the model for a meltdown cycle, just one phase, Agitation, is depicted to capture the process between the Trigger Phase and the most intense behavioral phase, Meltdown.

The primary value in classifying behavior in this way is to enable practitioners to understand the behavioral processes involved in an escalating cycle with discrete phases. The behavioral descriptions inform staff about what problematic behavior to expect at each phase of the potentially explosive behavior chain. The overall expectation is that once the behavior pattern has been identified, staff are in a much stronger position to intervene early and interrupt the behavior pattern before it escalates into a serious disruptive and unsafe situation. Moreover, evidence-based strategies corresponding to each of the six phases in the meltdown cycle can be readily identified so that service personnel can select appropriate strategies and develop intervention plans to address student behavior, wherever it is in the meltdown cycle.

This chapter presents a model for describing the cycle of meltdown behavior exhibited by students with ASD adapted from the acting-out behavior cycle developed and extensively implemented by Colvin (2004). The specific adaptations are derived from unique factors associated with the disability of ASD.

Model for Describing the Meltdown Cycle for Students With ASD

The details of this model have been generated from the our experience in observing and working with numerous students with ASD, their teachers, support personnel, and parents over the past 30 years and from reviewing research literature, published best practice procedures, and currently adopted evidence-based procedures. More recently, we have conducted several interviews with teachers, specialists, administrators, and parents, and have personally observed several classrooms to validate the model.

The specific phases of the meltdown cycle for students with ASD are presented in Figure 3.1: Six-Phase Model for the Cycle of Meltdowns of Students With ASD. Note that the graph rises as the behavior escalates to its highest level of intensity, meltdown, and falls away as the student behavior de-escalates. The escalating behaviors occur in Phases I through IV, followed by the de-escalating behaviors in Phases V and VI. In general, this conceptual model represents the interdependent behavioral dynamics of student behavior during an escalating and de-escalating episode of a meltdown.

  I. Calm

  II. Triggers

  III. Agitation

  IV. Meltdown

  V. Re-Grouping

  VI. Starting Over

Figure 3.1   Six-Phase Model for the Cycle of Meltdowns of Students With ASD

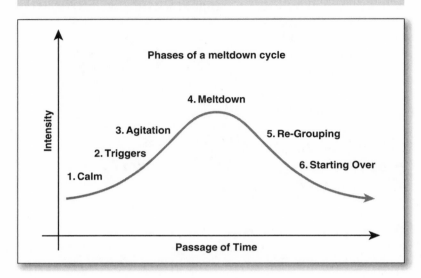

What follows is a detailed description of the behavioral characteristics of each of the six phases, a summary behavioral description of each phase, an illustration of each phase drawn from the examples of Ricky and Elena presented in Chapter 2 (Box 2.1), a summary checklist for the meltdown cycle, and a behavior support plan with case studies.

Note: The behavioral characteristics identified for each phase are generalizations from many students with ASD. It is imperative that teachers and service providers determine the specific or individual behaviors for their particular students for each phase in the cycle. The lists presented in this book are designed to serve as a guide or catalyst in making these determinations.

Phase I: Calm

Students who exhibit meltdown behaviors, even at regular intervals, have periods when they are quite calm, and to all outward appearances, their behavior is acceptable, generally cooperative, and responsive to the teacher's directions and expectations. Ideally, this is the situation that teachers, service providers, and parents would like to be the normal way of life for the students. An obvious goal would be to minimize or remove instances of meltdowns and maintain the students in a calm and cooperative state. This section presents information on the first phase of the meltdown cycle: Calm. The following topics are presented: (a) description of the Calm Phase, (b) list of common behaviors for this phase, (c) general behavioral descriptor, and (d) illustrations.

Description of the Calm Phase

Even though students with ASD can display very serious meltdown behavior, they also can exhibit moments when they are quite calm and appear to be content in the classroom. These periods of relative calm are considered to be the first phase of the meltdown cycle. In this phase the students can be responsive to teaching and learning and can be managed reasonably well in the classroom. Teachers often report that the student in this phase was having a good day; the level of behavior was such that the student was responding to, and was engaged in, the classroom activities. It is quite common at a staff meeting called for one of these students for a teacher to report, "Most of the time, [student's name] is a delight to have in the classroom, but at other times he or she is a totally different person and can be quite a handful." While there are limitations arising from the disability of ASD, in Phase I these students are generally able to function appropriately with other students in regard to sharing, working together, and getting along in general (given that ASD also includes students who are very low functioning and may have difficulty with staying on task, sharing, and responding appropriately in general). They are able to respond appropriately to praise and show interest and satisfaction in getting their work done and achieving their goals. Even though the students may have certain idiosyncrasies, and accommodations need to be made on a regular basis associated with the ASD disability, essentially their behavior is within the range of what is acceptable and can be managed in the classroom. Common behaviors for Phase 1 include the following:

Maintains On-Task Behavior. While some students with ASD may have less capacity than other students in the class for remaining on task, nonetheless they can maintain involvement in a task or activity with varying degrees of independence. The teacher is able to maintain instruction for this student and the rest of the class.

Engages in Tasks and Activities. With varying degrees of prompting and assistance, students with ASD who are in the Calm Phase can respond to instruction and become productively engaged in the particular class activity.

Follows Directions. Clearly, teachers need students to be able to follow directions for the general instruction and management of a classroom. Students with ASD are able to follow directions (some needing more explicit directions than others) when they are calm.

Permits Assistance. Many students with ASD have relatively low cognitive and social skills and often lack the ability to work independently. Consequently, they need constant assistance from teachers in order to engage in and complete tasks. When they are calm they are quite responsive and receptive to the levels of teacher assistance needed (later on, however, when the meltdown cycle begins, they are usually not receptive to assistance).

Makes Transitions Successfully. Transitions occur on a regular basis throughout a school day. When students with ASD are calm, they can receive the prompts or cues and make transitions successfully. Again, this responsiveness changes later on in the cycle.

Responds to Praise and Positive Interactions. Teachers know very well that students with high needs require a great deal of attention, recognition, and positive encouragement for their learning and behavior management. Students in this Calm Phase are typically quite responsive to positive feedback and approaches from their teachers.

Initiates Requests or Interactions. Even though some students with ASD may have quite limited communication and social skills, they can express their needs in ways that adults know what they are requesting. Similarly, they can express positive interactions so that staff know they are enjoying the current event or activity.

General Behavioral Descriptor

Summary of Phase I: Calm

Overall behavior is cooperative, focused, and acceptable.

Illustrations

Box 3.1 shows how Ricky and Elena functioned in the classroom in Phase I: Calm.

Box 3.1	Illustrations of Students With ASD in Phase I: Calm

Ricky	Elena
Ricky can stay focused on preferred items such as his Legos, puzzles, and computer programs. He can work with a teacher in a one-on-one situation but does not do well in groups. He enjoys writing and tracing letters and numbers. He can concentrate for long periods of time and can transition fairly smoothly when he has completed a task or project and a cue card is used. While he is not very responsive to teacher praise or positive contact, he seems to accept the contact especially if it is in the context of a task. He likes the high-five exchange and occasionally initiates it.	*Elena does best when teachers and staff respond to her interests. She likes to talk about her hobbies such as her card collection and talks with more animation when staff shows interest in her collection and what she is saying. She can stay focused for lengthy periods especially with tasks that are routine and have definite closure such as completing a page of writing or math.*
	She enjoys independent activities such as computer games and watching TV or video programs and games.
Main behaviors when Ricky is in the Calm Phase:	Main behaviors when Elena is in the Calm Phase:
1. Works well when left alone	1. Works best when teachers show interest in her work
2. Stays working once started	2. Talks about hobbies and interests
3. Accepts assistance, follows directions, and concentrates for long periods	3. Stays on task with set routines with definite closure
4. Can transition when previous task is completed with a cue card	4. Works well when left alone
5. Receives praise related to tasks	5. Stays focused with computer games

It is quite clear in each of these examples that both Ricky and Elena were calm and engaged in the classroom. The activities were engaging to them, and interactions were at a level they could accommodate.

Phase II: Triggers

Perhaps one of the greatest challenges in working with students with ASD is identifying the factors or *triggers* that cause a student to escalate. In some cases the triggers are quite evident. For example, a student with ASD may be fully engaged in an activity such as playing a game on the computer, and another student comes along and says, "My turn," and begins to move the keyboard. The student with ASD becomes very agitated, starts to make noises, and grabs hold of the keyboard, pushing the other student's hands out of the way. The other student stays. The student with ASD begins to scream and takes considerable time to recover. In this case the sudden intrusion by the other student disrupting the student with ASD was the trigger. However, in many cases the triggers are not so evident. For example, a student with ASD has an assistant on the bus when he is transported to school. One day this student begins to scream and pound on the back of the seat. The assistant is asked what set him off and the response is, "I have no idea. He just started yelling and flailing his arms. I had been watching him too. It just happened all of a sudden." Triggers for students with ASD can often be very difficult, if not sometimes impossible, to observe.

This section describes triggers so that teachers may be in a stronger position to identify what it is that sets off their student's behavior leading to meltdowns and thereby help to buttress against future occurrences of such meltdowns. The following topics are presented: (a) description of the Trigger Phase, (b) list of common triggers, (c) general behavioral descriptor, and (d) illustrations.

Description of the Trigger Phase

Triggers are defined as the events that set off the cycle of a meltdown. The student may be engaged appropriately in the first phase, Calm, and a trigger comes into play that sets the stage for a meltdown. In general, triggers are considered to be any factor internal or external that has the effect of disrupting the student's current state of equilibrium, taking the student from a calm to an escalated state. It is most important for teachers, service providers, and parents to pay particular attention to identifying triggers so that the environment may be adapted to minimize the effects of the triggers and the student may be prepared to manage the situations when they arise without escalation.

List of Common Triggers

The following list is meant to provide suggestions as starting points when teachers are trying to identify and address triggers. It may well be that in some cases teachers may have to continually search for operating triggers. Clearly, if the triggers can be identified, then steps can be taken to minimize their effects. If the triggers have not been identified, then the teachers need to keep searching and use additional strategies for preventing agitation (described in Chapter 6).

Disruption of Schedules and Routines. Students with ASD are often characterized by having restricted, repetitive, and fixed routines. When these routines are disrupted, students can become quite upset, which can lead to serious acting-out behavior. Classrooms are run by the school schedule, and teachers are expected to develop their own schedule of activities within set periods or time frames. In a sense, students with ASD have their own clock and their own schedule so that if the class schedule says, "Time's up," and these students aren't finished with an activity, they are disrupted, which can upset them and lead to problem behavior. Unplanned changes or surprises in schedules can also cause serious problems, such as a period has to be cut short because lunch time has been changed or a field trip has been planned. In general, any form of disruption or interruption of students' activities can lead to problems.

Novel situations can also cause serious problems. Any unfamiliar location, unrehearsed task, or new experience can trigger problem behavior.

Sensory Overload or Cravings. It has been very well documented that students with ASD are particularly sensitive to sensory conditions in their environment. The classroom can be too bright, which can trigger reactions. Recess or the cafeteria can be too noisy for them. Kitchen smells or gas odors can trigger reactions. Sudden changes in these sensory stimulus conditions can also cause problems, such as the lights being turned up or a particularly loud announcement coming over the public address system from the office. Individuals with ASD apparently have internal mechanisms that are disturbed through sensory overload or sensory cravings. The students then resort to an array of behaviors designed to restore their equilibrium, and quite often these behaviors are unacceptable. For example, a student may be working on a math puzzle when the principal makes an announcement over the PA. The student puts her hand over her ears and starts repeating certain words quite loudly. The student is doing her best to drown out the noise from the announcement. Meanwhile the repeated mumblings disturb the rest of the class. Another student may be craving sensory stimulation and begin to jump, spin, and pace, which may disturb the class.

Inability to Communicate Needs. Students with ASD often have deficiencies with their expressive language skills. For example, they can comprehend a story (receptive language) but have great difficulty in expressing information about the story. This expressive language carries over to behavior. Students often know what they need yet cannot express their need in ways that are understood by others. This, of course, leads to frustration, and the situation is exacerbated if the teacher makes several incorrect guesses at what the students need. The students' frustration then builds up, leading to a possible meltdown.

Inability to Understand. In a similar way, students with ASD often do not understand what is required of them, whether it be directions, classroom or school expectations, or standard norms in the classroom. As one teacher expressed it, "They do not understand the 'why' of things." When they are asked, or expected to do things, they often have difficulty because none of it makes sense to them. These situations can occur on a frequent basis in the classroom, causing tension to build up, potentially leading to a meltdown.

Conflicts. In general, the sources of student conflicts occurring at school fall into two broad categories: denial of something the student wants or needs and something negative inflicted on the student. Some students with ASD have limited communication skills, especially in regard to expressing what they need. For example, a student might start making noises because he is too hot. The noises disrupt the class, so the teacher tries harder to get the rest of the class to settle down and ignore the student making noises. The student's need is not being met, so he reacts further, which can lead to a meltdown.

In the second case, these students, who are easily triggered, are often provoked when something negative is inflicted upon them. Students with ASD often become targets for students who do not understand them and the complexities of ASD. Other students may playfully tease them, provoke them, or bully them, which can lead to an escalation of behavior. These negative interactions can readily lead to a meltdown.

Pressure. A school day can be viewed as a very high-demand situation in which students are expected to comply with a wide variety of directions and complete a number of often complex tasks during the course of the day. Students are expected to manage their time well, function independently in a number of situations, and often manage multiple tasks at the same time. In many cases, students with ASD have poor adaptive skills and have difficulty finishing an activity or handling multiple tasks such as putting things away and washing their hands to get ready for lunch within a 5-minute time frame. The seemingly ordinary demands of a school day can set the stage for panic, frustration, anxiety, and other emotional responses, resulting in unrest that leads to problem behavior.

Ineffective Problem Solving. Students with ASD generally have limited strategies for identifying sources of problems, generating and evaluating adaptive options, negotiating with others, and implementing plans accordingly. These students often apply the one ineffective strategy repeatedly or resort to angry reactive behavior. They have not learned how to solve problems systematically, and essentially they need formal and carefully designed teaching in these areas.

Facing Correction Procedures. Students with ASD often have their own way of doing things, so when a teacher tries to show them another way or correct their responses, they react and can exhibit problem behavior. Moreover, the students can actively resist correction procedures so that when the teacher persists with a correction procedure, the students escalate.

Motor Skill Activities. Students with ASD can have highly tuned fine motor skills for very specific tasks. Their performance level can amaze their teachers and classmates at times. However, their motor-planning abilities (sequence of movements required to complete an action) and their overall application of motor skills to new or different activities are frequently very limited or poor. Consequently, activities requiring a range of motor skills or adaptations of previously learned skills can set the stage for resistance and problem behavior. In addition, these students may have the component skills but fail to understand or show interest in the activity. Again, when the teacher persists with the activity, students with ASD may react. For example, a student has shown the ability to throw things. Yet in a physical education class the teacher is unsuccessful in teaching her to throw a baseball, and the harder the teacher tries the more student reacts or acts out. Another student may show fine motor skills in one area, such as assembling a puzzle, but have great difficulty with handwriting and copying activities.

Impact of Health Issues. It was noted in Chapter 1 that some students with ASD are afflicted with medical or health issues such as stomach concerns (constipation, stomachaches, diarrhea), sleep problems, eating issues, and emotional problems. These conditions can set the students on edge so that in a classroom or school situation it does not take much to upset them and precipitate problem behavior. Even simple directions or demands can trigger serious behavior when a student is suffering from some health concern. While the immediate trigger could be something in the classroom, such as a demand, the underlying issue is that the student has a health problem.

Spillover of Issues From Home. Similar to health issues, sometimes something happens at home that set the stage for problems at school. A student may have had a bad bus ride, had trouble with getting ready for school, or had to leave a special toy or game at home. Again, a simple demand or task at school can trigger serious problem behavior when the student is already upset from something at home.

General Behavioral Descriptor

Summary of Phase II: Triggers
Overall, student has trouble understanding and communicating.

Illustrations

Box 3.2 shows the triggers operating with Ricky and Elena in Phase II.

| Box 3.2 | Illustrations of Students With ASD in Phase II: Triggers |

Ricky	Elena
The students were milling around the front of the class making noise, and the teacher assistant approached Ricky for reading.	*The teacher directed her to put away her cards as it was time for class, saying that Elena could sort the cards later during break. Elena said to wait one minute and kept moving her cards around. The teacher moved toward her, knowing that she would play with the cards all day if permitted. The teacher said quite firmly that the cards needed to be put away now and pushed one of the cards toward the center of the desk.*
Four Triggers were possibly operating for Ricky:	
1. The movement when other students were crowding around the front of the class	Three Triggers were possibly operating for Elena:
2. The noise level from the front of the class	1. Being told to stop sorting her cards when she was not finished; interrupted routine
3. The approach of the teacher assistant	2. The teacher's persistence with finishing up
4. The transition from what Ricky was engaged in to reading	3. The teacher touching and moving one of her cards

Phase III: Agitation

Triggers have the effect of moving a student's behavior from Phase I: Calm to Phase III: Agitation. *Agitation* is a general term for behaviors that are typically emotionally based, such as being angry, upset, depressed, on edge, withdrawn, worried, disturbed, frustrated, or anxious. While it is often quite difficult to pinpoint the actual feelings a student with ASD may be experiencing, agitation is typically an observable manifestation that something is wrong for the student. Students often display high levels of agitation as a function of their inability to control or manage the triggers identified in Phase II.

Note: In some cases students with ASD, particularly younger students, may quickly accelerate from Phase II: Triggers to

Phase IV: Meltdown. These students skip Phase III: Agitation. Teachers often refer to these students as having a very short fuse. One of the students whose case is illustrated throughout this chapter, Ricky, was engaged with one of his favorite puzzles (Phase I: Calm). But because of the noise at the front of the room and the teacher assistant approaching him to move to instruction, he began screaming and flailing his arms immediately. He went directly from Phase I to Phase IV, skipping Phase III.

The Agitation Phase can last for a considerable amount of time, depending on which triggers are operating. Teachers may describe some students as "being on edge" and that it does not take much to tip them over the edge. Other students may take longer to escalate. In general, agitation can be manifested in one of two ways: responses indicating *increases* in behavior or responses indicating *decreases* in behavior. It is very important to note that the behaviors exhibited in this phase represent sudden changes from the behaviors in Phase I. If the student exhibits these behaviors habitually, then we are looking at a very different problem, such as hyperactivity, severe depression, psychotic conditions, or a dual diagnosis.

Increases in Behavior

Busy Hands and Feet. Students often display a noticeable increase in hand movements, such as pencil tapping, drumming their fingers, rubbing their thighs, opening and closing books, flapping their hands, and tugging at their clothes. Similarly, they become more fidgety, wiggling their legs and tapping their feet.

Repetitive Self-Talk. Students with ASD in this phase engage in repetitive self-talk such as repeating lines from a movie or TV show. The behavior is called *self-talk* because the students are not making any attempt to talk to another person. They simply repeat words, phrases, or expressions over and over again. This repetition has a high level of intensity, and it is often difficult for teachers to break up the perseveration or disengage the students from the talk. Some students, instead of using words repetitively, will begin to hum incessantly or make unintelligible noises. Other students will simply speak louder. The combination of loud and perseverative talk is a strong indicator of agitation.

Increase in Self-Stimulation. Students may switch from the task they are presently engaged in to begin self-stimulatory behavior such as twirling or spinning an object, rocking back and forth on the chair, incessant fingering of materials, and rubbing their thighs with their hands. For example, a student may be using a keyboard with both hands. Then she begins to wave one hand in the air, type with the other hand, then wave both hands, and begin typing again.

Low-Level Destructive Behaviors. Some students will break or tear items in class when they are upset. For example, they may tear up a piece of paper into a number of small pieces, break a wooden stirrer into a number of small pieces, or pull a thread from their clothing and begin to twirl it repetitively. Later in the meltdown cycle, these students may engage in more serious destruction of property when they are out of control.

Changes in Body Language. Some students will show increases in body language that reflect agitation and tension building, such as frowning, fidgeting in their seats, finger tapping, muscle tensing, rolling their heads from side to side, an overall stiffening of their body, or wiggling their feet.

Aimless Pacing and Wandering. Students may cease what they are doing in an activity and begin to wander around the room. They may begin to pace back and forth, walk in circles, or go to a corner and begin to rock back and forth. There appears to be little purpose or focus in their movements. It is as if they are drifting around the room. They may look at something or pick up an object and put it down. They act as if they do not know what they want or nothing seems to engage their attention for very long.

Cognitive Breakdowns. Some students will show changes in their ability to answer or ask questions. They may also have difficulties in being able to respond to academic tasks (reading, writing, math) when they normally can respond appropriately.

Stuttering. There may be difficulties with delivery of speech, especially in the form of stuttering, for some students. When they are calm, stuttering is not present.

Noncompliance. Here, students refuse to cooperate or strongly resist the teacher's directions. When the teacher tries to follow through with the request or direction, students show more resistance and opposition, which can readily escalate to a meltdown.

Whining, Making Noises, and Crying. This behavior typically prompts immediate teacher attention or assistance, which may escalate the situation.

Decreases in Behavior

Staring Into Space. Students may be tracking what is happening in class and then begin to stare vacantly. They appear to be daydreaming and staring into space. They look at something with a certain amount of concentration, but their minds are somewhere else. They may also appear to be deaf in that things are said to them but they do not give any indication that they have heard anything.

Veiled Eyes. Students will avoid eye contact by looking away or looking down. Similarly, they will pull their hat down over their eyes, pull up the lapels of their jacket, or sink their head as low into the jacket as they can. Some students with ASD exhibit these behaviors on a regular basis; however, when they become agitated they show more withdrawal than normal. Again, many students with ASD display these behaviors when they are calm. If they become agitated, these behaviors show marked increases.

Becoming Mute. While students with ASD often have limited language to begin with, they stop talking and refuse to communicate altogether when they are upset. When the teacher approaches them, they use avoidance techniques such as putting their head down, turning away, or looking into space in a vacant manner. In some cases a student's delivery is very subdued and difficult to hear. Again, the student is communicating that he does not want to engage in conversation or interaction.

Contained Hands. Students with ASD typically have busy hands. However, some students, when they are upset, may hide their hands by sitting on them, folding their arms, or putting their hands behind their back. Essentially, these students contain their hands as a strategy for disengaging from present academic tasks or classroom activities.

Withdrawing From Activity. In some cases students abruptly stop what they are doing, stand up, push items away from themselves, walk quickly away from the setting, stand in a corner, sit in another chair, or pace up and down. It is very clear they have lost focus on the activity at hand and are now looking very intense.

Seeking Isolation. A very common strategy for students with ASD when they are upset is to escape from the present situation that may be aversive to them. They run to a corner of the room, leave the room, crawl under a table, or hide in a cubbyhole or closet. This response is very common when they are bothered by noise or crowding (sensory overload).

General Behavioral Descriptor

Summary of Phase III: Agitation

Overall, student exhibits sudden increases or decreases in behavior.

Illustrations

Box 3.3 shows how Ricky and Elena functioned in the classroom in Phase III: Agitation.

| Box 3.3 | Illustrations of Students With ASD in Phase III: Agitation |

Ricky	Elena
Ricky is playing with his puzzle. There is considerable noise and movement at the front to the class. The teacher assistant approaches him to begin instruction. Ricky starts screaming very loudly and begins to flail his harms.	*The teacher directs her to put her cards away as it was time for class, saying that Elena could sort the cards later during break. Elena says to wait one minute. She puts her head down and starts moving the cards quickly and mumbles to herself.*
Ricky skipped Phase III: Agitation and went straight to Phase IV: Meltdown.	The specific signs of Agitation are evident from an increase in these behaviors:
	1. Putting her head down
	2. Moving the cards more quickly
	3. Mumbling or self-talk

Phase IV: Meltdown

Phase IV represents the most intense behaviors in the students' repertoire during the escalated cycle. Quite often the phase is referred to as *serious acting-out behavior, peak behavior, blow-ups, rage,* and *total loss of control.* Whatever it is called, people involved with students who exhibit this behavior know exactly what it is and certainly wish the occurrences were rare events. Generally, the students' behaviors are characterized by disruption so serious that class cannot continue or continues with great difficulty. In addition, meltdown behaviors often represent a threat to the safety of others and to the involved student. It is as if the student has snapped and becomes out of control. Meltdown behaviors typically include the following:

Serious Destruction of Property. Student meltdowns can result in substantial and costly damage to property. For example, students may trash a classroom, throw a chair across the room or through the window, kick holes in the wall, or push over bookshelves.

Physical Attacks. A student may lash out at another person, the teacher or another student, which could cause physical harm. These aggressive behaviors include punching, kicking, biting, throwing objects, hair pulling, and even more serious behaviors, including attacks with objects.

Self-Abuse. In this case the harmful behaviors are self-directed, as in face slapping, hitting, pinching, hair pulling, biting, head banging, and scratching the body. Significant self-injury could occur.

Severe Tantrums. These behaviors are very disruptive in the classroom and can include screaming, yelling, throwing objects, pushing desks over, and flailing on the floor. While students are engaged in these meltdowns, it is virtually impossible for the teacher to maintain instruction or to proceed with great difficulty. For safety reasons and to enable other students to receive instruction, adjustments are usually made in the classroom, such as moving the other students to an adjacent setting and leaving the student exhibiting the meltdown under the supervision of another adult.

Running Away. In many cases, when students are out of control there is the choice of fight or flight. Some students may simply take off to escape the situation and run out of the classroom and, in some cases, out of the school. Their departure is generally accompanied by explosive behavior such as yelling, cursing, banging doors, and kicking walls and furniture. These students can put themselves in precarious situations because their anger or loss of control may impair their judgment, especially if they run away into dangerous areas such a busy traffic intersections.

General Behavioral Descriptor

Summary of Phase IV: Meltdown

Overall, student is out of control.

Illustrations

Box 3.4 shows Ricky and Elena's behaviors in Phase IV: Meltdown. Each student has lost control, exhibiting serious disruptive and unsafe behavior.

Box 3.4   Illustrations of Students With ASD in Phase IV: Meltdown

Ricky	Elena
The students were milling around the front of the class near the teacher at the beginning of class. The teacher assistant approached Ricky as she worked one-on-one with him for language. Ricky jumped up, ran to the corner of the room, and started screaming. He sat on the floor, put his hands over his ears, and continued to scream, thrashing his legs. The teacher assistant sat beside him, and then Ricky ran off to another area of the room, continuing to scream. The teacher and another assistant took the rest of the students to an adjacent small room, leaving Ricky and the teacher assistant in the classroom	The teacher told her to leave her cards and that she needed to go to the time-out area and quiet down. Elena grabbed her cards and kicked the chair over on her way to the time out area, shouting that the cards were hers. The teacher followed her. In the time-out area, Elena began to pound on the walls, rip up materials, and kick the desk, screaming that the cards were hers. The teacher withdrew, watching her from a short distance. Behavior indicators of a Meltdown: 1. Grabbing cards 2. Kicking furniture

(Continued)

(Continued)

with the connecting door open. Ricky continued to scream and flail his arms, with the teacher assistant standing some distance from him. Behavior indicators of a Meltdown: 1. Sustained screaming 2. Running to the corner of the room 3. Falling on the floor 4. Thrashing his legs 5. Flailing his arms	3. Shouting and screaming 4. Pounding on walls 5. Ripping materials 6. Sustained screaming

Phase V: Re-Grouping

A teacher once said, "The only good thing about a meltdown is that it cannot last forever. It has to quit—even if it is through exhaustion." Phase V: Re-Grouping marks the end of a meltdown and the beginnings of recovery. The period can be best understood as a transition from being out of control to resuming normal activities. This phase can pose difficulties for the student and staff as the student is usually confused in emerging from a meltdown. Staff are often wary of intervening with the student during this phase as they worry they may trigger further escalation and the meltdown will resume. This phase is best characterized as a *reintegration process*; as the title of the phase suggests a re-grouping takes place. The student behavior is similar to Phase III: Agitation, in which there is a very clear lack of focus and obvious appearances of distraction and uncertainty. The following are common behaviors manifested in this phase:

Withdrawal. Many students will put their heads down and try to sleep; either they are trying to withdraw from the situation or they may be genuinely fatigued following a prolonged physical acting-out period during the meltdown. Or they may withdraw into their fantasy world. In other cases, they simply need to quiet down in order to think things through and regain their composure. Some students may react strongly when approached by an adult early in this phase. Their basic need here is to be left alone, and their reaction to being approached is to communicate that they want to be left alone.

Confusion. Immediately following a meltdown, students typically display confused, seemingly random behavior, such as wandering around the room, fidgeting, toying with items, staring at things momentarily, picking something up and then putting it down, holding an object in one hand and flapping the other hand, and sitting then standing. In effect, there appears to be a clear lack of focus in the students' behavior. They typically exhibit more distance than usual during this phase and are much harder to reach.

Reconciliation Attempts. Some students with ASD, who are relatively social to begin with, will want to make up or test the waters to see if the teacher still likes them or to obtain some relief from their confusion. They will offer to help or come close and stand near the teacher. Some may verbalize that they are sorry for what happened.

Denial. Students with ASD who have a solid grasp of language often become sullen and engage in denial responses during this phase. They are very quick to blame others or perseverate on their initial need, which in their mind has been denied. These students will avoid talking about the escalated serious behaviors and try very hard to hold the conversation around the triggers that caused the problems in the first place. Denial is very common when students believe that they were victimized during the initial triggers, which, of course, could be the case.

Responsiveness to Directions. Many teachers have found that students will cooperate, almost willingly, to very concrete directions such as "Michael, please sit on the bench over there." It appears that the students are very distracted at this point and a clear, concrete direction provides a needed focus. This responsiveness is related to another feature of this phase noted earlier—*confusion*. The directions from the teacher provide a focus for students and something to do.

Responsiveness to Manipulative or Mechanical Tasks. Students with ASD typically become actively involved with tasks or activities that are very mechanical, such as sorting things, leafing through magazines, or playing with toys such as Legos. These activities help them become focused and settle down.

Responsiveness to Special Interests. Some students with ASD have an especially strong or intense interest in certain areas or activities, such as natural science, science fiction movies and games, trains, and animals. These special interests may help them focus, relax, and settle down.

Avoidance of Discussion. At this point, some students with capacity to discuss and debrief will avoid discussion and opportunities to problem solve. In many cases they will utter repetitive statements that serve to block any form of discussion or debriefing. While debriefing and problem solving are very important (for those students capable of such interactions), it is usually better to wait until the students have calmed down and become engaged in the current class activity. The reason is that they will not be open to problem solving and the discussion will center on denial, blaming others, or avoidance by repetitive talk. The issue is timing.

Limited Coordination. During a meltdown, students often display high rates of hand flapping, shuffling feet, and thrashing on the floor. As they exit a meltdown, motor control and coordination recovery may be slow. For example, a student in transition from a meltdown may be involved with an activity on the computer. She may tap some keys with one hand and wave and flap the other hand and then vice versa. After some time she will become more coordinated and use both hands on the keys.

Note: Some students may have great difficulty in settling down and resuming class work and may be very slow to respond to strategies to assist them. In these cases more time must be allowed for them to regroup and settle down, as is discussed more fully in the next section.

General Behavioral Descriptor

Summary of Phase V: Re-Grouping
Overall, student withdraws and displays confusion.

Illustrations

Box 3.5 shows Ricky and Elena's behaviors in Phase V: Re-Grouping.

Box 3.5	Illustrations of Students With ASD in Phase V: Re-Grouping

Ricky	Elena
Ricky continued to scream and flail his arms, with the teacher assistant standing some distance from him. After about 5 minutes, the screaming subsided and Ricky sat on the floor with his hands over his ears. The teacher assistant waited a few more minutes and sat on a nearby chair. The teacher assistant put some Legos on the floor and began building a house, putting some Legos near Ricky. She then prompted Ricky to help with building the house and handed him some Legos. He took the items and began to assemble them.	*The teacher withdrew, watching her from a short distance. Elena eventually sat down, gathered her cards, and held them. She then sat in the corner, still very upset, and began to sort her cards. When she was finished, she folded her arms and stared at the floor for some time. The teacher approached her and gave her a form to complete that she did, but quite slowly. When she had completed the form she was directed to join the class, which she did.*

Ricky — Behavior indicators of Re-Grouping:

1. Screaming began to subside
2. Sat on floor with hands over ears
3. Responded to prompt to build with Legos
4. Built house of Legos.

Elena — Behavior indicators of Re-Grouping:

1. Sat down, still upset
2. Began to sort cards
3. Folded arms, stared at floor
4. Completed form
5. Cooperated with directions to join class

Phase VI: Starting Over

In this final phase, students returns to a nonagitated and relatively normal state (behaviors exhibited in Phase I: Calm). Essentially, they are able to participate, perhaps marginally, in instruction or the current classroom activities. They show a willingness to get going again but usually display some slowness or awkwardness in responding. In other words, the students are back on track but still display some uncertainty, anxiety, or irritation. Typically, when the students have been productively engaged in the class activity, and presuming they have the necessary cognitive skills, the teacher will conduct some form of debriefing to review the incident and provide some guided problem-solving plan for similar situations in the future. The following are specific behavioral characteristics of students with ASD in this phase:

Eagerness for Independent Work or Activity. Typically, students with ASD become engaged in, or may actively seek, some kind of relatively independent "busy work," that is, activities that they have already mastered and require active responses, such as coloring, looking up words in a dictionary and writing down the meanings, drawing, or writing. These activities need to be relatively easy and require little, if any, interaction with the teacher or other students.

Subdued Behavior in Group Work. While there is some interest in getting back on track, these students find activities that involve interactions with other students or staff very difficult (more so than normal). Strategies such as cooperative learning, or any activity involving working with others, would be very difficult for the students at this point. Many students with ASD are subdued in group work as a rule, but in this phase they are more subdued than normal.

Subdued Behavior in Class Discussions. Similarly, these students find it very difficult to contribute to class discussions in this phase. Also, when they are asked a question or are invited to comment, their responses are usually muted and cryptic.

Defensive Behavior. In this phase, as they are recovering from a serious episode, some students with high communication skills will display behavior that is cautious and almost measured. They may be confused or wary or simply have learned over the years that it best to be quiet at this time and say nothing.

Cautious With Problem Solving. It is common practice for teachers to debrief and problem solve with students, who have the necessary skills, once they are back in class and productively engaged. However, the students will more than likely show caution, hesitation, and perhaps mild resistance when the teacher tries to engage them in this way. Because students with ASD typically have difficulty with problem solving, they may need to be directly walked through the problem-solving sequence more slowly and perhaps more regularly.

Increased Focus. Students with limited language and intellectual skills will show increased focus on aspects of tasks. They will look at certain features longer, touch items, smell items, and appear to be exploring certain articles.

Increased Physical Calm. Students with ASD in general, and in particular students with low skills, will show an obvious calmness in the way they sit. They can hold positions longer, whether sitting or standing. Self-stimulation, if it is common, will resume but at a more controlled or steady rate compared to when students are upset. For example, they may be content to twirl something rather than spin it with intensity.

General Behavioral Descriptor

> **Summary of Phase VI: Starting Over**
>
> Overall, student is responsive to concrete tasks and reluctant to interact.

Illustrations

Box 3.6 shows Ricky and Elena's behaviors in Phase VI: Starting Over. These vignettes show the students are somewhat subdued but were able to cooperate and resume the current class activity.

| Box 3.6 | Illustrations of Students With ASD in Phase 7: Starting Over |

Ricky	Elena
The teacher assistant put some Legos on the floor and began building a house, putting some Legos near Ricky. She then prompted Ricky to help with building the house and handed him some Legos. He took the items and began to assemble them. The other students, the teacher, and the other teacher assistant reentered the classroom and continued with their spelling groups. Ricky then joined the group and sat quietly but did not participate. Behavior indicators of Starting Over: 1. Worked with the Legos 2. Followed direction to join the group 3. Sat in the group but did not participate	*Toward the end of the period, when Elena was engaged with the class, the teacher reviewed the form with her and addressed how she could have sorted her cards without the big scene. Elena mumbled a lot during the meeting but cooperated overall.* Behavior indicators of Starting Over: 1. Resumed class activity 2. Cooperated with debriefing 3. Was somewhat subdued and mumbled a lot

Summary Checklist of Phases in the Meltdown Cycle

Form 3.1: Summary and Checklist for Behaviors of Each Phase in the Meltdown Cycle provides an overview of the characteristic behaviors of each phase in the conceptual model of the meltdown cycle for students with ASD. The lists of behaviors for each phase are not meant to be exhaustive; rather, they are examples of the class of behaviors for that particular phase. The item "other" is included at the end of the list for each phase for the reader to add characteristics not included here.

Form 3.1   Summary and Checklist for Behaviors of Each Phase in the Meltdown Cycle (Appendix A)

Student Name: _____ Date: _____

Teacher: _____ Grade: _____

Phase I: Calm

Overall, behavior is cooperative, focused, and acceptable.

- ☐ Maintains on-task behavior
- ☐ Engages in tasks and activities
- ☐ Follows directions
- ☐ Permits assistance
- ☐ Makes transitions successfully
- ☐ Responds to praise and positive interactions
- ☐ Initiates requests and interactions
- ☐ Other

Phase II: Triggers

Overall, student has trouble with understanding and communicating.

- ☐ Disruption of schedules and routines
- ☐ Sensory overload or cravings
- ☐ Inability to communicate needs
- ☐ Inability to understand

☐ Conflicts
☐ Pressure
☐ Ineffective problem solving
☐ Facing correction procedures
☐ Motor skill activities
☐ Impact of health issues
☐ Spillover from health issues from home
☐ Other

Phase III: Agitation

Overall, student exhibits sudden increases or decreases in behavior.

Increases in Behavior	Decreases in Behavior
☐ Busy hands and feet ☐ Repetitive self-talk ☐ Increases in self-stimulation ☐ Low-level destructive behaviors ☐ Changes in body language ☐ Aimless pacing and wandering ☐ Cognitive breakdowns ☐ Stuttering ☐ Noncompliance ☐ Whining, making noises, and crying ☐ Other	☐ Staring into space ☐ Veiled eyes ☐ Becoming mute ☐ Contained hands ☐ Withdrawing from activity ☐ Seeking isolation ☐ Other

Phase IV: Meltdown

Overall, behavior is out of control.

☐ Serious destruction of property
☐ Physical attacks
☐ Self-abuse
☐ Severe tantrums
☐ Running away
☐ Other

(Continued)

(Continued)

Phase V: Re-Grouping

Overall, student withdraws and displays confusion.

☐ Withdrawal
☐ Confusion
☐ Reconciliation attempts
☐ Denial
☐ Responsiveness to directions
☐ Responsiveness to manipulative or mechanical tasks
☐ Responsiveness to special interests
☐ Avoidance of discussion
☐ Limited coordination
☐ Other

Phase VI: Starting Over

Overall, student is responsive to concrete tasks and reluctant to interact.

☐ Eagerness for independent work or activity
☐ Subdued behavior in group work
☐ Subdued behavior in class discussions
☐ Defensive behavior
☐ Cautious with problem solving
☐ Increased focus
☐ Increased physical calm
☐ Other

Source: Adapted from Colvin, 2004.

Behavior Support Plan

The six-phase conceptual model for the cycle of meltdown behavior allows us to develop a procedure for assessing the behavior of students with ASD and developing corresponding interventions. Form 3.2 (Appendix B) is a blank form providing a framework for developing an acting-out behavior support plan. This form is divided into two sections: (a) *Assessment,* in which the student's specific behaviors are identified for each of the six phases in the meltdown cycle, and (b) *Strategies* for managing each of the phases.

Form 3.2   Behavior Support Plan (Appendix B)

Student Name: _____ Date: _____ Homeroom Teacher: _____ Grade: _____ Staff Present: _____	
Assessment	*Strategies*
Calm	Calm
Triggers	Triggers
Agitation	Agitation
Meltdown	Meltdown
Re-Grouping	Re-Grouping
Starting Over	Starting Over

In order to develop a behavior support plan, it is common practice to call a meeting involving all staff members who have direct responsibilities with the student and the parents. It is recommended that each person complete the Summary and Checklist for Behaviors of Each Phase in the Meltdown Cycle (Form 3.1/Appendix A) prior to the meeting. At the meeting, the chairperson secures consensus from the group on the key behavioral descriptors for each of the six phases of the meltdown cycle and completes the assessment component of the Behavior Support Plan (Form 3.2/Appendix B). In Section II, corresponding strategies are described for implementation in each of the six phases of the meltdown cycle for both the school and home components.

Case Studies

Here, we illustrate how Form 3.2 can be used to develop a behavior support plan for students with ASD who display the meltdown cycle. The two case studies, Ricky and Elena, were first introduced in Chapter 2 (Box 2.1), and their characteristic behaviors for each phase in the meltdown cycle have been listed throughout this chapter in Boxes 3.1–3.8. At the meeting, staff and parents shared their responses to the checklist form (Form 3.1) and the chairperson completed the assessment portion of the behavior support plan (Box 3.7 for Ricky; Box 3.8 for Elena). Please note that *only* the assessment part of the plan, left column, is presented in this chapter and that the strategies component, right column, will be added in Section II. The parent component is presented in Chapter 10.

Box 3.7	Behavior Support Plan for Ricky

Student Name: Ricky Wiley	Date: 4/3/11
Teacher: Mary-Sharon Weatherspoon	Grade: 1
Staff Present: Josephine Wardley, Tom Scruggs, Ellen Hawthorne, and Mary-Sharon Weatherspoon	

Assessment	Strategies
Calm	**Calm**
Works well when left alone	
Stays working once started	

Assessment	Strategies
Accepts assistance, follows directions, and concentrates for long periods Can transition when previous task is completed Receives praise related to tasks	
Triggers The movement when other students were crowding around the front of the class The noise level from the front of the class The approach of the teacher assistant The transition from what Ricky was engaged in to reading	**Triggers**
Agitation Ricky skips Phase III: Agitation and goes straight to Phase IV: Meltdown.	**Agitation**
Meltdown Sustained screaming Running to the corner of the room Falling on the floor Thrashing his legs Flailing his arms	**Meltdown**
Re-Grouping Screaming began to subside Sat on floor with hands over ears Responded to prompt to build with Legos Built house of Legos	**Re-Grouping**
Starting Over Worked with the Legos Followed direction to join group Sat in group but did not participate	**Starting Over**

Box 3.8	Behavior Support Plan for Elena

Assessment	Strategies
Student Name: Elena Warner — Date: 6/18/11	
Teacher: Josh Parkinson — Grade: 10	
Staff Present: Angela Timms, Joe Barkley, Josh Parkinson, Marietta Coley, and Francis McMahon	

Assessment	Strategies
Calm *Works best when teachers show interest in her work* *Talks about hobbies and interests* *Stays on task with set routines with definite closure* *Works well when left alone* *Stays focused with computer games*	**Calm**
Triggers *Had to stop sorting her cards when she was not finished; routine was interrupted* *The teacher's persistence with finishing up* *The teacher touching and moving one of her cards*	**Triggers**
Agitation *Putting head down* *Moving cards more quickly* *Mumbling*	**Agitation**
Meltdown *Grabbing cards* *Kicking furniture* *Shouting and screaming* *Pounding on walls* *Ripping materials* *Sustained screaming*	**Meltdown**
Re-Grouping *Sat down still upset* *Began to sort cards* *Folded arms, stared at floor* *Completed form* *Cooperated with directions to join class*	**Re-Grouping**

Assessment	Strategies
Starting Over	**Starting Over**
Resumed class activity	
Cooperated with debriefing	
Somewhat subdued and mumbled a lot	

Chapter Summary

This chapter presents a six-phase model for describing the cycle of meltdowns for students with ASD. Behavioral descriptions for each phase in the cycle were selected from a large sample of students with ASD, covering all ages from kindergarten through high school, who exhibited this behavioral pattern. The primary purpose of classifying behavior in this way is to enable practitioners to understand the behavioral pattern involved when these students' behavior escalates to the point of a meltdown and slowly recovers. The behavioral descriptions inform staff about what problematic behavior to expect at each phase of this explosive behavior chain. The overall expectation is that once the behavior pattern has been identified, staff are in a much stronger position to intervene early and interrupt the behavior pattern before it escalates into a meltdown. The strategies or interventions corresponding to each of the six phases in the meltdown cycle are presented in the remaining chapters of this book.

SECTION II

Strategies for Managing the Phases of the Meltdown Cycle

In the previous section, a conceptual model was presented for describing the six phases of a meltdown cycle. In this section, information is provided on strategies designed to manage behavior in each of these phases. The basic idea is that once certain behaviors are observed in a particular phase, staff apply strategies identified for that particular phase. Since each phase represents a link in the behavioral chain, the basic approach is for staff to effectively manage the behaviors in the early phases. In this way the behavior chain may be interrupted, thus preempting the later phases in which the more serious behaviors occur. In the early phases, I through III (Calm, Triggers, and Agitation), emphasis is placed on teaching and prevention techniques. In the later phases, IV through VI (Meltdown, Re-Grouping, and Starting Over), the emphasis is on safety, minimizing disruption, follow-up procedures, and recovery.

4

Calm Phase

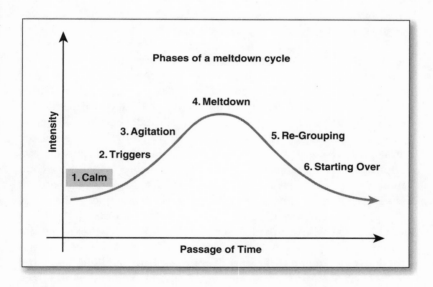

The goal in designing strategies for Phase I: Calm is to maintain all students, including those with autism spectrum disorder (ASD), who exhibit acting-out behaviors productively engaged with instruction and learning and to prevent any escalation of behavior—that is, to keep them in the Calm Phase. If students are on task, challenged, achieving academically, and successfully engaged in classroom activities, there will be less likelihood of serious behavior occurring. In this sense, quality instruction and a well-organized classroom that is especially tuned in to the needs of students with ASD are assumed to be crucial preventive measures controlling problem behavior. Moreover, if students have a serious incident, it is the specifics of the classroom structure and instructional practices that will largely determine whether the students may recover once the incident has been de-escalated and they return to the classroom activities.

There are typically three placement options for students with ASD: self-contained classrooms for students with ASD, special education resource rooms, and general education or mainstreamed classrooms. Consequently, teachers of students with ASD must be equipped to meet not only the educational needs of students with ASD but also the needs of other students in special and general education. This chapter builds upon what has been learned in the past two decades about how to establish a safe and positive classroom environment not only for students with challenging behaviors, including students with ASD, but *for all students* (Brophy, 1999; Ganz, 2007; Moran, Stobbe, Baron, Miller, & Moir, 2008). Because of the unique characteristics of students with ASD, as was discussed in Section I, additional strategies need to be incorporated for these students to be successful. In this sense the strategies presented in this chapter need to be seen as basic strategies applicable to all students. However, the difference is that these common strategies will have an overlay tailored for the particular needs of students with ASD. The following strategies are described: (a) manage the physical environment, (b) address sensory issues, (c) provide visual supports, (d) provide peer support, (e) establish expectations and rules, (f) implement routines, (g) provide a practical schedule, and (h) deliver instruction. The overall approach is to highlight the central ideas of each strategy, present examples, and recommended resources.

Manage the Physical Environment

Many behavior problems can be avoided by carefully managing the physical environment. The overall approach is to first address general classroom organization guidelines and to then describe specific accommodations for maximizing the successful integration of students with ASD into the classroom setting.

In today's classrooms, many functions take place. Some activities occur on a regular basis, while others occur infrequently. The success or failure of these activities in achieving their intended goals will, by and large, depend on the way in which the classroom is designed. Unfortunately, some classrooms serving high-needs students, including those with ASD, are quite small compared to the size of the standard general education classroom. Consequently, it may pose quite a challenge for the teacher who has a small classroom to accommodate the following recommendations. In these cases all we can do is to recommend that teachers adopt and adapt in ways that are workable for them. The following is a list of guidelines for classroom design common to all classrooms; it is followed by a summary checklist for organization of classroom space.

Independent Work Locations. These areas require minimum distractions. Select areas for independent work in a low-traffic section away from commonly used materials, time-out, quiet time, and free-time activity areas.

Group Work Locations. Arrange these areas to ensure that students can easily attend to the teacher and to each other. A semicircle or row configuration of desks can facilitate group-oriented instruction.

Choice Activities Centers. Choice activities are sometimes used for students who finish their work early or as a reward for special achievement. Restrict this activity to a quiet location behind the instructional areas. Establish specific rules of behavior for the use of these activities.

Quiet Time Area. This area is used to enable students to calm down when they experience stress or become agitated. Choose an area that is as isolated as possible to prevent interactions with other students and staff. This area is particularly important for students with ASD. Also be sure to select a location based on low sensory stimulation, especially with regard to noise and lighting.

Time-Out or Isolation Area. This area is used for students who need to be isolated in the classroom as a negative consequence for deliberate problem behavior, such as refusal to follow directions or hitting or hurting someone. Select an area that isolates the student from the other students in order to limit their interactions. This area could consist of a desk in the corner of the room, a small table facing the back of the room, or a desk at the side of the room.

Storage Materials and Supplies. These are located in low-traffic areas to avoid distraction and yet allow easy access. Ensure that materials are neatly arranged and that they do not obstruct supervision or the students' view.

Teacher's Desk. Place the teacher's desk out of the path and flow of instruction. In addition, be sure to locate the desk in an area that will safeguard personal property and confidential material.

Notice Board. Locate the notice board so that it is highly visible in the room and in a high-traffic area, but does not divert student attention during instruction. Also, regulate material posted on the notice board so that it is not too stimulating for students with ASD.

Remove Obstructions to Supervision. Maximize supervision by arranging the room so that all students are in sight. Be careful of high objects, such as bookshelves, that may obstruct supervision.

Flexible Seating Arrangements. The seating arrangement can vary considerably. The key is *flexibility.* In developing a seating plan, (a) ensure that all students can easily see presentations during whole-group instruction, (b) minimize distractions, (c) use clusters for group instruction, (d) involve students in the seating plans as appropriate, and (e) vary the seating arrangement on a periodic basis (rows, semi-circular arrangements, and clusters).

Organization of Classroom Space. Form 4.1: Organization of Classroom Space is designed to assist teachers in developing a classroom plan to meet their specific needs and to ensure that the major bases are addressed.

Form 4.1   Organization of Classroom Space (Appendix C)

Activity	Completion Date	Notes
1. Locate specific classroom areas for:		
a. Independent work	__/__/__	_____
b. Group work	__/__/__	_____
c. Choice activities	__/__/__	_____

Activity	Completion Date	Notes
d. Quiet time	__/__/__	_____
e. Time-out or isolation	__/__/__	_____
f. Storage materials and supplies	__/__/__	_____
g. Teacher's desk	__/__/__	_____
h. Notice board	__/__/__	_____
i. Remove obstructions to supervision	__/__/__	_____
j. Other	__/__/__	_____
2. Design flexible seating arrangements:		
a. Rows	__/__/__	_____
b. Clusters	__/__/__	_____
c. Semicircular	__/__/__	_____
d. Combinations	__/__/__	_____
e. Other		
3. Identify other classroom design tasks and functions:		
_____	__/__/__	_____
_____		_____
_____		_____
_____		_____

Address the Sensory Issues

In addition to the strategies listed above for managing the physical environment, students with ASD need adjustments to address sensory stimulation concerns in the classroom. We have noted that one of the defining characteristics of this population is their sensitivity, particularly their overreactivity and underreactivity to sensory stimulation. Auditory, visual, tactile, olfactory, proprioceptive, and vestibular stimulation may significantly interfere with these students' ability to concentrate in the classroom and to maintain their composure. In order to help these students, give careful consideration to controlling the levels of sensory stimulation that occur in the classroom. A summary of common sensory issues is presented in Box 4.1: Common Sensory Issues, which is followed by a description of common classroom adjustments that are made to address these issues and a summary checklist, Form 4.2: Checklist of Adjustments for Sensory Issues.

| Box 4.1 | Common Sensory Issues |

Overreactive	*Underreactive*
Auditory	
• Overly sensitive to noise • Distracted by background noise • Holds hands over ears when noisy • Humming, singing, incessant talking	• Does not respond to name • Oblivious to surrounding sound • Grinds teeth, pulls ears • Creates constant sounds
Visual	
• Bothered by bright lights and sun • Covers eyes • Distracted by movement or shiny objects	• Unaware of other people • Unable to locate desired objects • Loses sight of moving people
Tactile	
• Does not like being touched • Does not like to touch certain textures (clay, water, paint, rough clothes) • Dislikes certain food textures	• Needs to touch and feel objects • Puts objects into mouth • High threshold for pain

Overreactive	Underreactive
Gustatory and Olfactory	
• Overreacts to certain smells	• Sniffs objects and people
• Gags and/or refuses food	• Licks objects
• Refuses medications	• Does not notice strong smell
Proprioceptive and Vestibular	
• Overreacts to movements	• Rocks constantly
• Walks close to walls	• Generally slow to move
• Clings to supports such as banisters	• Head banging and biting
• Always spinning or moving	• Prefers sedentary activities

Adjustments for Auditory Stimulation

Be aware that many students with ASD struggle with a wide variety of sounds. Some of these sounds we might label annoying; others may seem pleasant to us but unbearable to them. Students with ASD not only have problems processing speech but also have extreme difficulty when the room is full of competing sounds. Make adjustments to reduce classroom noise, such as putting carpet remnants under chairs, approaching students to talk to them rather than speaking loudly across the room, and limiting the use of music. In many classrooms, fans are used during the hotter months, which raises the noise level of the classroom. Student with ASD could wear headphones that have noise reduction capacity for activities that generate a lot of noise or when they are engaged in independent activities. Be on the alert to prepare the students for occurrences of loud intrusions such as the school bell or announcements over the public address system. Ask the following questions when assessing sound or noise issues: Which sounds are difficult for the student? How can I modify the environment? How can I reduce classroom noise in general? Can some sounds be changed? Can the student be moved to a quieter location? Can headphones be used effectively? How can I prepare the student ahead of time for some intrusive sounds (for example, the school bell and announcements)? How can I teach the student some coping strategies to deal with sound problems?

Another important area of auditory concern is the noise level related to lighting. The combination of flickering and humming from fluorescent lighting is a common problem area for individuals with ASD. Try turning off the overhead lights for one day to see if this helps your students with ASD. If this is a problem, at the very least have new ballasts and lights installed in the classroom.

Adjustments for Visual Stimulation

Most classrooms are highly decorated, especially in elementary schools, to promote a bright, positive, and stimulating environment for learning. But certain arrangements may visually distract students with ASD and, in some cases, overwhelm them. Moving stimuli like mobiles, pets in a cage, or bright fish in an aquarium may cause distraction and problems. This does not mean the classroom has to be dull and unstimulating, but be aware of specific items that may be especially distracting to these students and make adjustments accordingly

Place items that may be overstimulating to students with ASD in more isolated areas of the room so that they are accessible to other students and less likely to trigger the students with ASD.

Adjust for Tactile Stimulation

Many individuals with ASD do not like to be in crowded situations where they are likely to be accidentally bumped or touched. Control congestion as much as possible, especially when students are entering and exiting the classroom. Keep high-traffic areas such as supply cabinets and pencil sharpener locations free from congestion. Similarly, make sure that students' desks are away from these areas. Students with ASD may become frustrated from other students bumping into their desk or just being in their space as they move in these areas.

Note: Be aware that the lunchroom and assemblies are high-problem areas because they are not only crowded but also noisy. Sensory overload is highly likely unless adjustments are made. Make accommodations for students with ASD by allowing them to sit in a more isolated area during an assembly and to go to lunch early to avoid the noise and crowding.

Adjust for Gustatory and Olfactory Stimulation

Some students with ASD have difficulties with the aromas of perfumes, aftershave lotions, and colognes. Contact the parents or previous teachers to determine if there are olfactory issues related to certain products. Given this information, make adjustments such as talking with adults who work in the classroom (teachers, assistants, volunteers, and regular visitors) about limiting the use of these products. Also be aware of other potential problem scents, including scented markers, candles, science experiments, art supplies, and scented stickers. If need be, seat students with ASD near a window or allow them a small personal fan in order to minimize these odors or odors from the cafeteria. In addition, some students may have problems having lunch in the cafeteria because the odors are too strong. Or the problem may be one of limited food preferences by the student. Make other arrangements in these cases as needed.

Adjust for Proprioceptive and Vestibular Stimulation

Some students have difficulty being aware of where they are in space. For example, they bump into objects or walls, not realizing these objects are present. This problem is generally called *proprioception* or *position sense* (Molloy, Dietrich, & Bhattacharya, 2003). Other students crave stimulation and sensations arising from the need for an unusual amount of movement. For example, they rock, swing high, jump, pace, and spin. This issue is called *vestibular* or *balance sense.* It is important to continually keep informed of the potential conditions that may cause problems and make adjustments as necessary.

Recommendation. Both proprioceptive and vestibular problems are generated by *internal stimuli* or needs as distinct from the sensory issues identified above, which are driven by external stimuli such as lighting, noise, and odors. For this reason, the stimuli are hard to identify. We strongly recommend that an evaluation be conducted by an *occupational therapist* to identify the extent of sensory issues and to develop specific recommendations for adjustments that can be made in the classroom and at home.

Classroom Adjustments for Sensory Issues. Form 4.2: Checklist of Adjustments for Sensory Issues is designed to help teachers identify sensory issues for their students in order to make adjustments in the classroom as appropriate. The form is completed to illustrate its application; a blank version of the form is presented in Appendix D.

Form 4.2   Checklist of Adjustments for Sensory Issues (Appendix D)

Sensory Issue	Adjustment Options	Date Completed	Notes
Auditory	Reduce classroom noise Use headphones Develop quiet area Prepare student Other	__/__/__	
Visual	Use dimmers Reduce lighting Reduce visual distraction Other	__/__/__	
Tactile	Control congestion areas Minimize high-traffic areas Locate student's desk in low-traffic area Be aware of touching issues	__/__/__	
Gustatory	Identify preferred foods Offer choices for snacks Offer menu for lunch	__/__/__	
Olfactory	Monitor and reduce body scents, aftershave lotions, perfumes, and colognes Provide small fan Seat student near open window Be aware of scented supplies (stickers, etc.)	__/__/__	

Sensory Issue	Adjustment Options	Date Completed	Notes
Proprioceptive and Vestibular	Develop plan with occupational therapist Use rocking chair and mini-trampoline Provide physical space	___/___/___	
Other Sensory	Monitor temperature	___/___/___	

Provide Visual Supports

Students with ASD are visual learners as a rule. Because of this, visual supports serve an important role in educational programming for these students. Teachers frequently use visual aids to support academic learning—to improve understanding, develop new social skills, and enhance language skills. Visual supports can also be used to help students who exhibit challenging behaviors by providing structure to their day, helping them with transitions, improving their understanding of social situations, and teaching them to self-manage their behaviors.

Visual Supports That Provide Structure

Visual aids such as schedules, mini-schedules, or task organizers can provide structure to students' day by presenting information about when and how to perform what is required of them. For example, an activity schedule can give students information on the schedule. The schedule could be for a day, week, or month and be designed for the whole class, a group of students, or an individual student. A mini-schedule is a more detailed look at a given time period and provides information about the activities that will occur within this time period. For example, a student who is having difficulties with the transition from the classroom to the lunchroom is given a mini-schedule outlining the sequence of tasks she needs to do before going to lunch—put away materials, push your chair in, wash your hands, line up at the door, and wait for the signal to leave for the lunch room.

Visual Supports for Transitions and Change

Students with ASD have an especially difficult time with transitions. Give these students an advanced prompt or cue so that they can anticipate the transition to a new activity. Some teachers use specific signals, such as chimes or special music, to indicate that an activity will end shortly and that the students need to get ready for the next activity on the schedule. Sometimes a timer is used as a visual cue to signal how long students have to make the transition. Commonly used timers include electronic devices, kitchen types, and commercial applications for use with computers.

Another reason students with ASD find transitions difficult is their rigidity or obsession with the need to complete tasks or activities. However, in many cases an activity may need to be completed later, and the delay can cause problems. In these cases, break the task or activity into smaller segments, choose an end point for one of the segments, and communicate to students that the other segments will be completed at the next scheduled time.

Other useful tools are a timer or countdown cards, which can be used to provide a visual signal that the task is nearing completion. Also take advantage of the effective strategy called *first-then cards*. Present two cards with a visual for what is to happen now, *first,* and what is next, *then.* For example, point to the first card saying, "First, lunch," and then point to the second card saying, "Then, computer."

Use Visual Supports for Managing Emotions and Behaviors

Teachers employ a variety of visual strategies to help students self-manage their behaviors and control their emotions. The idea is that the visual cues help students communicate what they need and also provide information on what is required of them. In this way their needs are met and expectations are clarified for them. Consequently, emotional outbursts and problem behavior due to frustration are reduced. For example, some students with ASD have problems taking turns, and simple turn-taking cards can be developed with the words or picture "My Turn" on it. Or a student may have a problem waiting. To teach the behavior of waiting, have the student make a request and then have him hold a card with a symbol, picture, or the word "wait" on it. Then tell the student to wait and praise him for waiting. Then as occasions arise throughout the day when the student needs to wait, use the same routine with the "wait" card.

Another important skill that can be addressed with visual supports is making choices. Students are often required to choose an activity or to respond to a need such as using the restroom, having some more milk at snack time, or using the quiet room. To teach this skill start with a card with two choices on it, and gradually expand the number of choices until a choice board is developed. Choice boards can be used to help students communicate what they need and what they prefer, which in turn helps them manage their emotions and deal with stressful situations.

Develop a Visual Support System

In this section, we describe four steps for developing a system of visual supports, followed by Form 4.3: Illustration of Steps for Developing a Visual Support System. A blank version of this box is presented in Appendix E.

Step 1: Identify areas of the school day where visual supports are needed. Given that there is a wide range in communication needs for students with ASD, it is critical to pinpoint where the students need assistance. For some students transitions may pose problems, and for others it may be details for completing a task or making a request. The system needs to be tailored to the unique needs of each student. For high-needs students the system must address all aspects of the school day.

Step 2: Select the type of visuals to be used. Typically, the visuals are drawn from photos, pictures, drawings, icons, or written words. Visual aids can range in complexity from simple and concrete to complex and abstract depending on the students' understanding level. For example, real objects are the most concrete form, followed by color photographs, color then black-and-white pictures, line drawings, graphic symbols, and finally written language—the most abstract form. In addition to written words, use pictures, photographs, and symbols to communicate with students, such as letting them know what they will be doing next, where to go, and how to behave. Similarly, use visual cues to help students identify the beginning and end points of an activity and to help them understand the directions involved in a lesson.

Step 3: Collect the needed symbols. Gather whatever material is readily available for generating the symbols to be used, and use the variety of resources from published and online material, some of which are free. (See Box 4.4: Resources for Visual Supports). In addition, where possible, take your own digital pictures by following these simple guidelines: (a) identify the critical elements of the picture, (b) shoot close up, (c) eliminate the background, (d) monitor the lighting, and (e) take generic photos (Hogdon, 1995).

Step 4: Create and package the visual supports to be used. Organize the visual supports into a system for ready access. Ensure the system developed has the characteristics of portability, durability, clarity, and age-appropriateness.

Form 4.3   Illustration of Steps for Developing a Visual Support System

---

Student Level: This system is designed for an elementary student with ASD who is verbal and moderately intellectually impaired.

Step 1: Identify areas of the school day where visual supports are needed

The student has trouble with most transitions from period to period and with moving activities outside the classroom, such as recess and lunch.

Step 2: Select the type of visuals to be used

The student has very limited reading skills (words, abstract images, and drawings will not serve the student). It was decided to use pictures from current magazines for the type of visual support system.

Step 3: Collect the needed symbols

Collect a variety of current magazines from home and the school library, as available. Pay particular attention to the detail of the pictures to ensure they are not cluttered with other information and clearly depict the key concept.

Step 4: Create and package the visual supports to be used

Cut out pictures and paste them on letter-size cardstock for ease of filing and transporting. Maintain folder of pictures for additional needs and adjustments.

Resources

Given the range of needs for students with ASD, it is important for teachers to have at their fingertips readily accessible material and resources. Box 4.2: Resources for Visual Supports presents a list of commonly used and recommended resources that could be used as a starting point as the teacher builds a bank of materials and resources.

Box 4.2	Resources for Visual Supports

Books

Hogdon, L. A. (1995). *Visual Strategies for Improving Communication: Practical Supports for School and Home.* Troy, MI: QuirkRoberts.

Quill, K. A. (1995). *Teaching Children With Autism: Strategies to Enhance Communication and Socialization.* New York, NY: Delmar.

Savner, J. L., & Miles, B. S. (2000). *Making Visual Supports Work in the Home and Community: Strategies for Individuals With Autism and Asperger Syndrome.* Shawnee Mission, KS: Autism Asperger.

Online Resources

Autism Speaks interactive module: www.autismspeaks.org/family -services/resource-library/visual-tools

Autism Internet Modules: www.autisminternetmodules.org/user_mod.php

The Geneva Centre for Autism: http://elearning.autism.net/visuals/main.php

Free Online Pictures and Clip Art (Numerous sources are available)

http://acobox.com

www.classroomclipart.com

Commercial Software

Mayer-Johnson offers Boardmaker Plus, a very popular program that uses icons. This computer program offers literally thousands of symbols (www.mayer-johnson.com).

Different Roads to Learning is a company that has materials, including visual supports, for teachers who work with students with autism (www .difflearn.com).

Silver Lining Multimedia sells materials for making photo schedules and other visual supports (www.silverliningmm.com).

Provide Peer Support

Social interactions between students with ASD and their peers tend to be quite minimal compared to interactions between nondisabled students. Additionally, students with ASD are often subject to teasing and bullying, and are excluded from many activities as a result of their limited social skills.

One very important strategy for increasing positive social interactions between these students and their nondisabled peers, and for minimizing problems, is to develop a system of *peer supports* (National Research Council, 2001). A comprehensive peer support system usually includes (a) peer awareness training, (b) peer networks, and (c) peer tutoring (Carter, Sisco, Chung, & Stanton-Chapman, 2010).

Conduct Peer Awareness Training

Both classroom and schoolwide education about ASD have beneficial effects for both the students with ASD and their nondisabled peers (Baker, 2003). At the schoolwide level, conduct specific activities to heighten awareness, such as celebrating diversity on certain days with displays, assembly announcements, posters, and pamphlets providing information about ASD (and other groups). Similarly, at the classroom level hold discussions, conduct role plays, and organize displays and projects to provide essential information about the disability of ASD. Be sure to address these questions: What is ASD? How do students with ASD act? What are some of the difficulties these students have? Why do they act this way? What causes ASD? How can you help? (See www.bridges4kids.org/pdf/Growing_Up_Booklet.pdf.)

Develop Peer Networks

A peer network is an established, structured social group that provides support for students with disabilities by promoting social interactions within the classroom and school (Thiemann-Bourque, 2010). The goal of a supportive peer network is to increase positive attitudes among students throughout the school. Additionally, the network provides a natural structure for students with ASD to have opportunities to learn a variety of age-appropriate social responses (Thiemann-Bourque, 2010).

Incorporate Peer Tutoring

Peer tutoring is a commonly used strategy for teaching social behaviors to students with ASD (National Research Council, 2001). Teach the peers how to be *play organizers,* where they are taught how to share, help, give affection, and praise in a play situation with students with ASD (Goldstein, Johnson-Martin, Goldman, & Hussey, 1992). In addition, teach the peers how to initiate interactions, respond to targeted students' social initiations, and act as tutors in school activities, including academic instruction, lunchtime, recess, and recreational activities (Krebs, McDaniel, & Neeley, 2010; Owen-DeSchryver, Carr, Cale, & Blakely-Smith, 2008).

Establish Expectations and Rules

There is no question that students with ASD need highly structured, well-organized, and consistently managed classrooms. These students need to clearly understand what is expected of them not only in the classroom, but also in any area of the entire school where they are expected to function. Carefully address these three areas of rules and expectations: (a) schoolwide rules, (b) classroom expectations, and (c) specific classroom rules.

Schoolwide Rules

These rules apply to all students and to all school settings, including hallways, classrooms, cafeteria, playgrounds, school buses, library, and gymnasiums. The rules usually fall into three main areas: (a) *school safety* (e.g., walking, no running, in the hallway; cell phones turned off and no text messaging when in the classroom), (b) *order* (e.g., talking quietly and no yelling in the hallways, responding appropriately to school bells), and (c) *standards* (e.g., follow the dress code, no smoking on school property). These regulations are typically listed in the student handbook, and, in general, schools take specific measures to ensure that the rules are systematically taught throughout the schools (Colvin, 2007). However, the procedures used to teach the schoolwide rules to all students are usually inadequate for students with ASD. These students need more specific instruction with much more detail (see section Systematically Teach the Rules).

Classroom Expectations

These are the universal guidelines for behavior that are designed to help students become successful in school, especially with their learning, such as acting responsibly, being cooperative, getting along with others, using good manners, making an effort, doing one's best, expressing feelings in an appropriate way, and making good choices. Expectations, by their very nature, are general and are frequently too vague and abstract for students with ASD to fully grasp and act upon. Provide specific instruction to ensure adequate understanding. Use many examples (both positive and negative examples) to demonstrate what the expectations look like, and provide multiple opportunities for practice and feedback. Examples are listed in Box 4.3: Illustration of Classroom Expectations.

Box 4.3	Illustration of Classroom Expectations

1. Be responsible

2. Be safe

3. Cooperate

4. Do your best

5. Respect others

Specific Classroom Rules

Rules are the concrete applications of the general classroom expectations. For example, being responsible is a common classroom expectation, while a corresponding rule would be to finish up on the computer when it is someone else's turn. Present rules in a way that informs the student both what to do and what not to do. For example, show the students how to "walk" and "not to run" in aisles; "put their materials away before recess" and "not leave their materials spread out on their desk or table"; and "raise your hand" and "not shout out" when you need to speak.

Selecting the Rules

Select rules that focus on student behavior that facilitate instruction, learning, and desirable behavior. The rules should be clear, observable, and measureable. In general, the fewer rules the better, especially for students with high needs. See Box 4.4: Illustration of Common Classroom Rules.

| Box 4.4 | Illustration of Common Classroom Rules |

1. Raise your hand, and wait until you are called

2. Treat your neighbors with respect

3. Follow the schedule

4. Work quietly

5. Follow directions

Students with ASD usually find that the combination of written words and symbols or cartoons help them understand and remember the classroom expectations and rules (Cohen & Sloan, 2007; Hogdon, 1999). Post the rules once they have been established, and, again, make good use of visual supports as necessary.

Systematically Teach the Rules

At the beginning of the school year and at regular times thereafter, the ideal is for the principal, administrators, building teams, and all teachers to make a concerted effort to teach and maintain the school-wide rules and expectations. The goal is to ensure that the rules are taught to all students, monitored, and frequently reviewed. This practice is especially important for those teachers who have students with ASD in their classroom. Teachers report that even though these students are rule governed, the biggest issue is that they often do not understand the rules—where and how the rules apply; the purpose of the rules; the many variations; and the range of application. Students with ASD are very prone to interpret things literally and will then misapply the rules. For example, the teacher may teach the rule of walking in the hallways by having students practice walking in the hallways and not running. However, when students are in the gym for PE and are required to run from one end to the other, they walk. In effect, the students have over-generalized the rule of walking in the hallway to all settings.

In teaching the rules, especially to students with ASD, introduce the full range of application of examples to clarify the settings where the rules do and do not apply. Take care to explain to the students exactly what the behaviors look like with modeling, practice, and use of visual supports as needed. Be very clear on where the rules apply and where they do not (that is, the *dos* and *don'ts*), for example, they are not to run in the hallways, but it is fine to run at recess.

Given that there is often a significant range in age and ability levels of not only students with ASD, but students in general, it is definitely a challenge to come up with a way to teach expected behavior to all students. However, there are *key steps* for teaching behavior that are based on general instructional practices used to teach any skill to students, including academic, social, and behavioral skills (Colvin, 2002; Sprague & Golly, 2004; Sprick & Garrison, 2008).

Teaching Rules and Expectations to Elementary Students

In general, there are five steps for teaching classroom expectations: (a) explain, (b) specify student behaviors, (c) practice, (d) monitor, and (e) review. These steps are described below, followed by an illustration in Form 4.4: Illustration of Plan for Teaching Classroom Expectations to Elementary Students. A blank version of this plan is included in Appendix F.

Step 1: Explain. Provide adequate reasons and purposes for the particular classroom procedure. Make provisions for discussion to clarify the need, provide an opportunity for student input, answer questions, and develop strategies to ensure the students understand the rationale for the expectation.

Step 2: Specify Student Behaviors. Clearly specify the behaviors that are required of the students. These behaviors should be *discrete*, *sequential*, and *observable*. The level of detail will vary according to the students' capacity to know what is required of them.

Step 3: Practice. Conduct practice sessions with the students to develop *fluency* in adhering to the rules and expectations in the classroom (in much the same way as skill development in other areas). Schedule practice sessions based on the amount of practice needed, as some students need more than others. Avoid requiring students to exhibit the classroom procedure independently in the real situation until they have demonstrated proficiency in the practice sessions.

Step 4: Monitor. Once the students have had the opportunity to practice the classroom procedure, the next step is to provide them with opportunities to exhibit the classroom procedure independently in the real situation. Students need close monitoring and feedback, especially in the early stages. Be sure to monitor the students with ASD during quiet work times and provide them with feedback on how they did. Again, make the feedback very specific, for example, "You worked very quietly during study time. You didn't make any noise at all." Finally, take extra steps to explain the *why* of the rules and expectations to ensure that the students understand the reasons for the rules.

Step 5: Review. Develop a system to periodically review the students' performance on the classroom procedures. Include formal observation of the students' behavior to assess how students are following the classroom procedures, how long the procedure takes, and what kinds of errors are occurring.

Note: More structure is usually needed for younger students, large groups of students, and classes comprising students with significant needs.

In general, keep in mind that students with ASD need explicit and concrete presentations of the rules and expectations, otherwise they may not fully understand what behaviors are expected of them (Attwood, 2007; Kluth, 2009). Also, it is usually necessary to spend some additional time specifically teaching the rules to these students in order to ensure understanding compared to other students.

Illustration

Form 4.4 presents an illustration of a plan using these five steps to teach an elementary-level classroom the expected behavior of *cooperation—following the teacher's directions.* A blank version of this plan can be found in Appendix F: Plan for Teaching Classroom Expectations to Elementary Students. The plan is designed for teaching the expected behavior to the whole class as a first step. If additional steps are needed for high-needs students, in this case students with ASD, these steps are added within these main steps denoted by the subheading "Student With ASD."

Form 4.4   Illustration of Plan for Teaching Classroom Expectations to Elementary Students

Expected Behavior: Cooperate—follow the teacher's directions

Student Level: Student has low skills in the areas of verbal expressive and receptive language. Teacher uses visual prompts most of the time to communicate directions and tasks.

Step 1: Explain

There are many students in the class. Everyone needs to have the chance to learn, get along with others, and feel comfortable in the classroom. It is very important for all students to follow the teacher's directions.

Student With ASD. Use a series of prepared visuals for the student with ASD as necessary, showing students engaged in an activity, the teacher talking to the class and then the students engaged in another activity.

Step 2: Specify Student Behaviors

When a teacher gives a direction, students are asked to stop what they are doing and listen, then begin to follow the direction within a few seconds.

Student With ASD. Prepare a visual showing students engaged in an activity. The next picture shows the teacher saying something, with all of the students watching. The next picture shows the students moving to another activity.

Step 3: Practice

Tell the class that they are going to practice following directions. Ask the students to begin writing. Say something like "Everybody, listen please." On this cue the students are expected to stop writing and look at you. Thank them for listening, and ask them to put away their materials and take out their reading book. The students begin to put their writing materials in their desk and take out their reading books. Acknowledge their promptness in following the directions.

Student With ASD. Again, visuals are prepared beforehand. The first one is labeled "Practice," with a picture of a student writing. The student is prompted to write. The next picture shows the teacher talking to the class. The student is prompted to stop writing and look at the teacher. The next picture shows students putting materials in their desk, which the student does. The final picture shows students reading. The student takes out a reading book and begins to read. Give the student a high five for following directions.

Step 4: Monitor

After the practice session for following directions, watch the students carefully when directions are given in class, especially to see if they stop what they are doing, watch you, and then follow the directions reasonably quickly. Acknowledge the students when they follow these steps.

Student With ASD. In the same way, observe the student with ASD when visual cues are presented to see if he stops what he is doing and then follows the direction communicated by the visual cue. Acknowledge the student when the steps are followed.

Step 5: Review

Provide feedback throughout the day on how the students performed in following directions. Acknowledge the students if a high level of cooperation was obtained. Provide reminders on the steps if the class responses were not highly cooperative. If the steps are not followed after reminders are given, then schedule more practice on following directions.

Student With ASD. Similarly, if cooperation with following directions is high, acknowledge the student strongly. If the standard or response is not high, then present the visual cues for directions more slowly and provide more emphasis on the steps (to stop what you are doing, listen, then follow the direction). If the student is still having problems, provide more direct practice sessions on following directions

*Teaching Rules and Expectations
to Secondary Students*

The main difference between teaching behavior to secondary students and elementary students is that there usually is less need for the practice step at the secondary level (Step 3 above). The teaching plan for older students reduces to three steps: (a) remind, (b) supervise, and (c) provide feedback. An example of an instructional plan to teach an expectation for secondary students is provided in Form 4.5: Illustration of Plan for Teaching Classroom Expectations to Secondary Students. Additional steps are usually needed for the high-needs students, in this case students with ASD. These additional steps are noted in the plan under the subheading Student With ASD. A blank version of this plan is presented in Appendix G.

Form 4.5   Illustration of Plan for Teaching Cooperation to Secondary Students

Expected Behavior: Following teacher's directions. The high school teacher is concerned that the class is taking too much time in making transitions within the block period for social studies.

Student Level: Student with ASD is reasonably competent but tends to be very literal when it comes to interpreting teacher directions and information. Teacher usually has to take extra steps to ensure student has understood information.

Step 1: Remind

The teacher explains to the students: "You are taking too long to switch over to new activities when I ask you to make a change. I appreciate that you are cooperating with working on tasks, but I need you to switch to other activities as well so we can cover everything we need to learn. So here is what I am asking you to do. I will make an announcement such as 'Listen, everybody, please.' When I say that I am asking you to stop what you are doing and look at me. Then I will tell you what I need to have you do next. You are then asked to make the switch to the new activity. So basically, when I call on the whole class, I am asking you to stop what you are doing, listen to the directions, and make the switch more quickly."

Student With ASD. The teacher approaches the student with ASD after class is engaged in an activity and goes over the details to make sure the student clearly understands. "Now when I say, 'Listen, everybody, please' you are asked to stop what you are doing and look up at me. I then tell you what's next, and you make the change immediately. I will tell you what can be done if you are not finished. Now you tell me what I am asking you to do." If need be, the teacher may practice the routine with the student.

Step 2: Supervise

The first thing the teacher does when calling on the class to announce a switch in activities is to watch to see if the students stop what they are doing and look up to listen. The teacher then checks that they move reasonably quickly to the next activity.

Student With ASD. Pay particular attention to the student with ASD as she probably has difficulty in stopping what she is currently doing.

Step 3: Provide Feedback

Provide brief feedback on how the students cooperated with the request to quicken their switch to new activities in class. Reiterate that it is hard to stop what they are doing to listen, and mention how responsive the students were to stopping what

> *they were doing to listen to the new directions. Pinpoint where improvement still needs to occur as appropriate.*
>
> **Student With ASD.** Give the student some individual or private feedback. This student may take longer than most of the class to make this change.

Implement Routines

Teachers at all levels of the K–12 system, in both general and special education, establish classroom routines as a fundamental strategy to ensure the smooth running of their classrooms. There are many benefits to instruction and management once a teacher has established the classroom procedures and routines, such as students learning self-management skills, instructional time being managed more efficiently, disruptions being minimized, and the classroom assuming a relaxed and orderly environment very conducive to teaching and learning. Familiarity with classroom routines is absolutely essential for students with ASD. These students, more so than most students, need the predictability and security that routines afford them.

Classroom routines refer to those procedures that are completed by students with minimum assistance from the teacher. Essentially, the goal is to have the students manage these tasks independently. These classroom procedures usually consist of a number of sequential behaviors or steps tied to specific activities conducted in the classroom. For example, a teacher may expect the students to turn in completed assignments and products at a specific place in the room or return to their desk and begin another activity without prompting from the teacher. Similarly, the teacher may require the students to raise their hand and wait quietly if they need help,

Essentially, classroom routines are simply a set of specific expectations directly related to student tasks and responsibilities. Consequently, use the same five instructional strategies for teaching classroom expectations described earlier in this section (*explain, specify student behavior, practice, monitor,* and *review*) for teaching routines. Again, with all forms of instruction and management, pay particular attention to how these routines are taught to students with ASD in order to ensure their understanding and mastery (usually more time and practice is needed). Make use of visual supports, as needed, to signal that a particular routine is to be followed and the explicit steps involved in correctly performing the routine.

It is particularly helpful to make a list of the routines to be established in the classroom. Develop your own list of classroom routines with appropriate levels of detail to suit your students' purposes and needs. The critical step, especially for students with ASD, is to be quite clear on the behaviors expected of the students in completing the routines. As with classroom rules and expectations, systematically teach the routines very early in the school year and constantly monitor and review the students' throughout the school year. See Box 4.5: List of Common Classroom Routines.

Box 4.5	List of Common Classroom Routines

- Entering the classroom
- Starting the period
- Working independently
- Securing attention
- Organizing and managing assignments
- Conducting tests and quizzes
- Speaking in class
- Moving around the classroom
- Establishing class helpers
- Obtaining supplies
- Using the restroom
- Using the water fountain
- Meeting special needs
- Using filler activities

Source: Colvin and Lazar, 1997.

Provide a Practical Schedule

Developing a practical schedule is one of the surest strategies for establishing a stable and predictable classroom environment for learning and appropriate behavior. Cotton (2003), in an extensive review of research literature, reported that schedules should be regarded as *flexible time-management tools* for teachers that are designed to best serve the educational needs of students. However, it is no easy task to develop a schedule since there are many blocks of time that have to be accommodated, such as lunch time, recess, core subjects, elective subjects, specialist's periods, team teaching periods, and district events. Be sure to allow priority time at the start of the school year before the students return in order to develop a workable and reliable schedule.

Typically, secondary teachers have little flexibility in developing a schedule in relation to the master schedule as the periods or blocks are determined by the master schedule based on subjects. Given that most secondary schools have adopted block scheduling involving 90- to 120-minute periods, carefully schedule the breakdown of activities within each block of time to maximize learning and minimize problem behavior. On the other hand, as a rule elementary teachers have more opportunity to construct a schedule after the schoolwide activities (recess, lunch, and so on) and specialist's periods have been identified.

Regardless of level, secondary or elementary, pay particular attention to ensure that the students with ASD comprehend their schedule and are able to operate with what you set up for them. Make good use of visual cues and other supports as needed to help these students follow the schedule. For example, daily schedules for students with ASD can be either written, visual, or a combination of both. At the most basic level, use objects or photographs to depict the sequence of activities. For the more able students, develop written checklists so that these students independently check the details of the schedule. Working with, and managing, the schedule is a great tool for helping students manage their time and, most important, manage transitions.

Deliver Instruction

Instructional Challenges

Students with ASD have a number of distinct difficulties that can inhibit learning, such as these:

- problems focusing on relevant information
- trouble tuning out distractions
- undue reliance on rote memory
- preoccupation with details and missing the main point of what is being taught
- deficits in problem-solving skills
- lack of organization
- problems with the generalization of newly taught material
- deficits with incidental learning (being overdependent on explicit and direct instruction)
- literal interpretation of teacher directions
- slowness in processing new material relative to other students (Minshew & Goldstein, 1998; D. L. Williams, Goldstein, & Minshew, 2006)

In effect, there is a substantial need for ongoing specific instructional modifications for learners with ASD. The following strategies, while not exhaustive, provide teachers with some practical suggestions that have proven helpful in delivering instruction to these students:

Be Clear and Concrete. Take steps to consciously present information in a concrete and specific fashion. Make the instructions explicit and direct. Use clear and unambiguous language. Try to keep the sentences simple, and frequently use repetition. Take care to give the students time to respond given that they may be processing the information more slowly than the other students in the class. For some students with ASD, it may be necessary to speak more slowly in order to give them time to process new information. Some students may need an individual presentation of directions and information using visual supports.

Use Direct Speech. Remember the students with ASD have a difficult time with nonliteral language such as metaphors, irony, and humor. These students are typically very literal, so forms of indirect information are difficult for them to understand and increase the chances of misunderstanding. As a rule, use direct speech and avoid indirect speech. From time to time reflect on the language you and other adults use with the students to assess the use of direct and indirect speech. Box 4.6: Illustrations of Direct and Indirect Communication presents some common examples of indirect communication along with corresponding examples of recommended direct speech.

Box 4.6	Illustrations of Direct and Indirect Communication

Indirect Communication	Direct Speech
I have a bone to pick with you.	I need to talk to you.
Don't rock the boat.	Leave things the way they are.
You have my word.	I will do it.
Could you get the box on the table?	Please get the box on the table.
Maybe.	I do not know.
You are the greatest.	This _____ is very good.
I've got something up my sleeve.	I have a plan.
Are you a little off color?	Do you feel sick?

Present Information One Modality at a Time

Many students with ASD have difficulty following instructions that are presented simultaneously (Bogdashina, 2003; Grandin, 2002). For example, a teacher may say, "Look at the picture, and see if you can see the whiskers on the cat." The student is required to look at the picture (visual) and follow the directions (audible). Or the teacher may be providing instructions for a report and asking the students to read the paragraph at the same time. This situation can cause sensory overload and confusion from having to deal with auditory and visual information at the same time. Students with ASD typically process only one modality at a time. Since the majority of these students are visual learners, present visual information first with a clear break before presenting audible information. The rule is to present one modality at a time. If a direction involving two or modalities is presented to the whole class, then it is usually necessary to repeat the direction using one modality at a time to the student with ASD.

Keeping Students On Task

When students are on task, clearly there is more chance for both learning and desirable classroom behavior to occur. Conversely, when they are off task, or are slow to get started, problem behavior often arises. A list of common strategies used by teachers is presented in Box 4.7: Strategies for Keeping Students on Task.

Box 4.7	Strategies for Keeping Students on Task

- Establish an entry activity and prompt students to engage quickly
- Make initial explanations brief and concrete
- Secure all students' attention before giving explanations
- Avoid interrupting the students once they are on task
- Reinforce students when they are on task in a way that is brief and oblique so as not to distract them
- Plan for difficult transitions
- Use direct speech
- Avoid dead time
- Have next task ready once initial task is completed
- Settle students down at the end of the period (Colvin, 2004)

Curriculum Intervention

Finally, one of the most serious consequences for students with the disability of ASD is that they end up lacking skills in so many areas that are essential for success in school and later on in life. These skill areas include, but are not limited to, academics, language and communication, social interactions, emotion management, practical living, and leisure and recreational activities. When students lack skills in these areas and become exposed to situations in which the skills are to be used, they often are left out, fall behind, or are otherwise significantly restricted. These limitations can become powerful triggers for problem behavior. The students may exhibit various forms of avoidance behavior or become frustrated and act out, possibly leading to a meltdown. There is no quick fix for addressing these triggers arising from skill deficits. Essentially, the students need to be systematically taught the required skills. This teaching typically requires instruction based on curricula that are well designed and research based (Arick, Loos, Falco, & Krug, 2005).

To begin with, *accurately* assess the students' skill levels in academic areas. If the assessment is inaccurate and these students are placed in content that is far beyond their skill level, they are very likely to become frustrated and will display problem behavior. Accurate assessment is necessary to determine the level of proficiency attained by these students and the logical place to begin instruction in a given domain. If the assessment is not completed, or completed inaccurately, the students will become frustrated because they cannot do the work, and problem behavior will arise. Or if the work is too easy, problems will still arise because the students become bored.

While teachers and specialists working with students with ASD are familiar with the multitude of curricula available to serve these students, questions arise as to how they might go about selecting the most appropriate curricula for their students. Given the wide range of skill deficit areas of students with ASD, establish some objective guidelines to assist in selecting which curricula to adopt and implement. We advocate very strongly that curriculum design for teaching students with ASD needs to be carefully selected, and along with several other authors and researchers, we have found that criteria need to be carefully used in the selection process (Aspy & Grossman, 2008; Commons & White, 2003; Flores & Ganz, 2007, 2009). Carefully consider the following questions in the process of selecting appropriate curricula and programs for your students, especially those with ASD:

1. Does the curriculum have direct application with research to show its effectiveness for students with ASD? (The curriculum may work for other students, but does it work for students with ASD?)

2. Is the design of the curriculum based on sound principles with adequate attention to key structural variables:

- Are skills carefully sequenced to make sure that the students learn the basic subskills?
- Are teaching procedures specified in enough detail to assist in the presentation of the content?
- Are correction procedures carefully specified?
- Is sufficient practice provided?
- Is previously covered material systematically reviewed? (Engelmann & Carnine, 1991; Mesibov & Howley, 2003)

3. Does the curriculum require a reasonable amount of training for teachers to implement the program?

4. Is the cost reasonable so that other necessary items for the classroom can still be purchased?

5. Is the approach sustainable?

6. Is the approach generalizable or limited to the specific curriculum?

7. Is the approach reasonably compatible with other programs either within the classroom or in mainstreamed settings?

Chapter Summary

Students with ASD who display acting-out behavior leading to melt-downs often have periods during which they are calm, can function adequately, and can obtain a measure of success with their learning. A major goal in teaching these students is to *keep them in this phase*. A crucial strategy for accomplishing this goal is to provide a classroom environment that is based on sound practices for all students and, in particular, accommodates the specific characteristics and needs of students with ASD. Teachers who create stable, positive, and predictable classrooms with a strong focus on quality instruction and learning are more likely to maintain their students in this Calm Phase and preempt problem behavior.

This chapter describes key strategies to help teachers organize the classroom environment and maximize instruction and student engagement, thereby increasing the learning opportunities for all their students. These strategies center on managing the physical classroom environment, establishing rules, implementing structure and routines, providing visual supports, providing peer support, establishing classroom rules and expectations, delivering quality instruction across the array of content areas, and selecting appropriate curricula. The basic approach is to use research-based and best-practice procedures for all students, with additional adaptations for students with ASD. These strategies, once implemented effectively, are more likely to keep the students in the *calm* phase and thereby maximize their learning and prevent problem behavior.

5

Trigger Phase

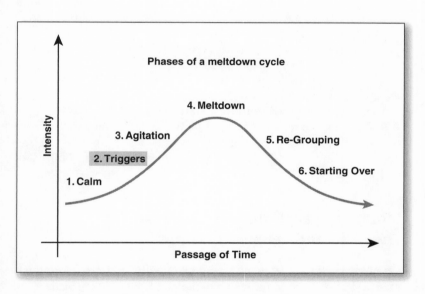

Phases of a meltdown cycle

4. Meltdown

3. Agitation

2. Triggers

5. Re-Grouping

6. Starting Over

1. Calm

Intensity

Passage of Time

S tudents with autism spectrum disorder (ASD) who exhibit meltdown behavior may function reasonably well in the classroom for
several periods of time, and we need to take every measure possible
to keep them at this level, Phase I: Calm. However, certain events

called *triggers* come into play that set the stage for problem behavior. As we saw in Chapter 3, which presented the six-phase model of a meltdown cycle, these triggers may be specific events, a result of cumulative events, or tied into skill deficits in the areas of communication, understanding, cognition, and socialization. These triggers can occur at school, outside the school setting, or in some combination of both settings. Moreover, the triggers can be immediate events or events that occurred earlier (from home, on the bus, in walking to school, or walking to the classroom). The effects of events that occurred earlier carry over to the classroom situation. Clearly, if the triggers are identified and effectively managed, there will be less chance of escalation in the first place. However, if they are not identified or addressed satisfactorily, then it is only a matter of time before the student's behavior will escalate.

The following strategies are designed to remove or weaken the effect that triggers have on student behavior, thereby decreasing the chances of a meltdown occurring and increasing the chances of the student being able to function successfully in the classroom. An illustration is provided with each strategy involving a student with ASD. The strategies are (1) modify the environment for sensory overload and sensory cravings, (2) provide visual supports, (3) prepare for the unexpected, (4) prime desired behaviors, and (5) adapt instruction.

Modify the Environment for Sensory Overload and Sensory Cravings

One of the defining triggers for students with ASD is sensory overload and sensory cravings (Murray-Slutsky & Paris, 2005; Sicile-Kira, 2004). Teachers, specialists, and parents are very cognizant of the role sensory overload and sensory cravings can play with these students' behavior.

Sensory Overload. Excessive noise, bright lights, strong aromas or odors, and congested settings where physical contact is inevitable can trigger problem behavior and lead to meltdowns. Teachers usually pay close attention in the classroom and throughout the school for situations in which sensory overload is likely to occur, and they make adjustments accordingly. Typically, modifications are made in the environment to control for sensory overload related to lighting, noise levels, congestion, and, in some cases, odors (see Box 5.1: Illustration of Modifying the Environment).

Box 5.1	Illustration of Modifying the Environment

Enrico is very sensitive to noise, and his teacher already had him use head-phones during breaks when he was playing independently. He predictably has trouble with the noise levels in group work, especially when there are several groups operating at the same time in the classroom. He holds his hands over his ears and mumbles when group instruction is underway. The teacher wanted Enrico to experience group work, so she made the decision to modify the environment. She rearranged the classroom so that the groups were more spread out and Enrico's group was somewhat isolated from the rest of the class. In addition, Enrico was positioned in the group so that he could not see the other groups. With the new arrangement the teacher noticed that he stopped putting his hands over his ears during group work. By arranging the room to minimize noise levels and reduce visual stimulation from other groups, she was able to help Enrico function better during group work.

Sensory Cravings. As noted earlier some students have a need for internal stimulation (vestibular and proprioceptive issues), which is often met through repetitive movement such rocking, spinning, and pacing (Bialer & Miller, 2011; Kranowitz, 2005). Teachers can meet this need and at the same time minimize the distraction in the classroom by having a designated area where the student may experience repetitive movement such as using a rocking chair, a large bouncing ball, or a mini-trampoline.

Provide Visual Supports

Students with ASD often have problems with communication and with understanding what is required of them. Miscommunication and misunderstanding can frequently serve as triggers for problem behavior. Providing cues for students is one of the most common strategies used by teachers when assisting with communication (McClannahan, & Krantz, 2010). A cue is a prompt, usually a visual signal such as a picture or something written on a slate, that is used to provide directions to the student. It is common practice to use such visual cues prior to transitions, when choices are presented, and for explaining and following the class schedule (Earles-Vollrath, Tapscott Cook, & Ganz, 2006). Given that students with ASD typically have communication problems, the visual cues help them communicate more reliably and reduce the chances of miscommunication or misunderstanding (see Box 5.2: Illustration of Providing Visual Supports).

Box 5.2	Illustration of Providing Visual Supports

Michael has no verbal language and has just finished instruction on beginning language. It is break time for him. The teacher puts three pictures in front of him and says, "It is break time Michael. Touch what you would like to do." She holds up each picture saying, "Legos, computer, or coloring?" Michael touches the Legos picture. He then proceeds to get the Legos basket.

Prepare for the Unexpected

Some of the most common triggers for agitation and meltdowns are unforeseen sudden changes in the environment, novel situations, or surprises. For example, a student may have swimming lessons at a set time each day, and on this particular day the pool is closed for cleaning. Or a student is always picked up after school by her mother, but on this day another family member, her aunt, arrives to pick her up. Logically, it is difficult to prepare students for these unexpected events, which is tantamount to *planning for the unplanned.* However, here are some strategies teachers use to provide some readiness for or tolerance of sudden changes:

Develop and Rehearse Plan B

Conduct rehearsals for key routines, which if disrupted are likely to cause a meltdown. Make a list of important routines for the student, and select a set phrase to prepare the student for changes. For example, if the student is collected each day after school before the end of the day, sit with him, use whatever language is appropriate, and say, "If your Mom is not coming today, someone else will be coming." Or if the student loves going to the gym for physical education, just before gym time rehearse with him, saying, "If we do not go to the gym today, we will be staying in the classroom for free time." Then if a change actually occurs, use the same phrase with the student, notifying him of the change. Some teachers use a stock phrase as a lead-in for all rehearsals of change, such as "If there is a change today in . . ."

These changes in the normal routines can be quite devastating for the student. Even though the occurrences are infrequent, it pays to provide regular rehearsals of an alternative plan to lessen the surprise element of such changes.

Rehearse for Novel Situations

Novel situations are those events or situations that the student has not experienced before that can trigger meltdowns (such as a class field trip to an apple orchard or playing a new game in class during the break). Again, conduct verbal rehearsals with set cues to help reduce the impact of this new situation. For example, rehearse the event with the student by saying something like "Today we are doing something different . . ." Use visual cues as needed to communicate that a change will be occurring. The basic idea is to increase the student's tolerance for change and the idea that change is coming.

Respond Quickly to Surprises

Clearly, teachers cannot be expected to anticipate or prepare the student for all the surprises that may occur during the course of the day. However, have your *antennae up* and be ready to respond very quickly should a surprise or novel situation arise. Move very quickly, and gently guide the student to a highly preferred or special interest activity at the moment a surprise is recognized. Hopefully, this preferred activity will serve to distract the student and interrupt the meltdown cycle.

Systematically Vary Routines

Another way to lessen the chance of changes to a routine triggering a meltdown is to carefully vary the routines. In this way the student may become less dependent on the rigidity of a routine or more tolerant of changes to a routine. However, pay particular attention to how much the routine can be changed, otherwise this strategy may induce agitation leading to a meltdown. The rule is to introduce changes very slowly in very small increments, with one change at a time, and monitor the student closely to catch any unrest or agitation. Generally, target routines that are not so rigid with the student first, and then target the more rigid ones later on once the student becomes comfortable with the changes (see Box 5.3: Illustration of Systematically Vary Routines).

Box 5.3 Illustration of Systematically Varying Routines

> Serena always sits in the same seat at the same table next to the same students each day for lunch. Over a period of several days, the teacher makes one change at a time, first switching the position of the two students opposite Serena, then on another day switching the ones next to her, then mixing up the students' seating, then having Serena sit in a different chair with the same students next to her, and so on.

Prime Desired Behaviors

Priming is a common procedure to prepare someone or something for some desired outcome. Painters prime homes for painting. A basketball coach primes a team for the finals. Priming is also an effective strategy for enabling students with ASD to perform certain desirable behaviors, especially when they are likely to exhibit undesirable behavior. Teachers use several variations of priming strategies to increase the chances of obtaining desirable behavior from their students, especially in contexts where inappropriate behavior is more likely.

Precorrection

Precorrection is one of the simplest and perhaps the most effective priming strategies for managing triggers in school and classroom-based situations (Colvin, 2005; Colvin, Sugai, & Patching, 1993). This strategy is based on knowing the triggers that set off the problem behavior and *intervening before* the student is exposed to these triggers. Essentially, *anticipate* problem behavior and act beforehand (see Box 5.4: Illustration of Precorrection).

Box 5.4 Illustration of Precorrection

> Isaac loved to play games on the computer. The teacher found that he became very resistant to ending his turn on the computer and had seen meltdowns associated with his refusal to finish his turn and to go to the next activity, especially when the next student badgered him to move. The triggers were transitioning from a highly preferred activity to group work and the presence of another student pressuring him to finish. The teacher made adjustments to address these triggers. First, when Isaac's time was

about to finish on the computer, the teacher approached him, told him he had 3 minutes left before group work, pointed to the diagram for group work on his schedule, asked him to repeat what is next, and set the timer for 3 minutes. She also told the next student to always stay back until Isaac had moved from the computer. The teacher provided strong praise for Isaac when he moved to the group after his timer went off (and to the student who held back).

Behavior Rehearsal

We have seen that the majority of students with ASD are skill deficient in many areas involving social interactions, communication, receptive and expressive language, fine motor tasks, and cognitive areas of thinking (such as making inferences, abstractions, or generalizations). Classroom activities throughout the day provide the students with constant exposure to these skill areas. Given the deficiencies in these skill areas, tension, frustration, and sometimes fear can arise, leading to problem behavior.

Use the strategy of behavior rehearsal to practice the targeted skills beforehand so that when the student is required to perform the skill she is more likely to be successful because of the practice (Schrandt, Buffington, & Poulson, 2009). This rehearsal, in a controlled setting, makes the student more comfortable, fluent, and confident with whatever skill is needed so that when she is engaged in the normal activity she is more likely to participate successfully (see Box 5.5: Illustration of Behavior Rehearsal).

Box 5.5	Illustration of Behavior Rehearsal

May has Asperger syndrome and has particular problems in participating in whole-class activities such as discussions. She interrupts other students when they have not finished and speaks very loudly. When she is corrected, she begins to pout, and depending on how her day has been, she may begin to act out and escalate.

Her teacher had the class working independently and took May, along with two other students, to a corner of the room 10 minutes before social studies began, which involved class discussions. The teacher told the three students that they were going to practice how to discuss in class and that

(Continued)

(Continued)

there were two rules. First, you wait until someone finishes talking before you speak. Second, you speak just loud enough so people can hear in the group. The teacher then provided practice for the three students on the two rules using two of the students as role models for May. May was given reminders about the two rules and was given very positive feedback when she followed the rules. When the practice session was completed, the teacher directed the class to get ready for social studies. Before class began she reminded the students of the two rules and complimented all students, especially May, when they followed these rules.

Behavioral Momentum

This strategy is adapted from Newton's Laws of Motion, which describe the phenomenon that once an object is set in motion it is relatively easy to keep it in motion. In the classroom, once a student is cooperating and productively engaged with one task, there is more chance of the student cooperating and engaging in the task that immediately follows (Kern & Starosta, 2004). This strategy also has wide application for students who have difficulty following directions (Belfiore, Pulley Basile, & Lee, 2008). Moreover, the strategy is particularly helpful for students with ASD who display avoidance behavior when difficult or less favored tasks are presented. Essentially, present fast-paced, easy tasks to get the student responding, and then slide into the harder task (see Box 5.6: Illustration of Behavioral Momentum).

Box 5.6	Illustration of Behavioral Momentum

Michael does not like to trace letters as part of his writing program. He typically taps the pencil in the desk or drops it on the floor when writing begins. The teacher sits with Michael and asks him to count to 10, which he does. Then the teacher gives him a high five, and Michael responds with a grin. The teacher asks him to open his writing book, which he does, and then says, "Let's count together to 15," which they do, followed by high fives. The teacher then asks Michael to take the pencil, which he does. The teacher says, "Let's write together," and traces the first letter, saying, "Now your turn, Michael. Trace this letter," pointing to the second letter. Michael traces the letter. They exchange high fives and continue this alternating turn procedure. The teacher fades out her turns, having Michael trace more and more letters. This routine is followed at the start of writing for several days, with the teacher doing less and less and Michael doing more and more of the tracing.

Adapt Instruction

Given that students spend a greater part of their day receiving instruction, different aspects of instructional delivery can serve as triggers for problem behavior. Reduce the effects of these triggers by using a number of strategies centered on varying instructional delivery. That is, change the way information is presented to students. Many strategies have proven effective in general education for securing and maintaining student attention during instruction. These strategies, with some adaptations, are also commonly used in delivering instruction to students with ASD to help them become productively engaged with their learning and at the same time facilitate appropriate behavior: (a) maintain the flow of instruction, (b) increase opportunities to respond, (c) ensure fast pacing, (d) provide necessary prompts, (e) shape responses, and (f) intersperse tasks.

Maintain the Flow of Instruction

When a student exhibits off-task behavior during instruction, ensure that the very first response is to *maintain the flow of instruction*, unless of course safety issues or severe disruption are involved (Colvin, 2005). There is always the chance that the student may be redirected to the particular instructional activity. Whereas, if instruction is stopped, then the students' off-task behavior may be reinforced, making it harder to resume instruction (see Box 5.7: Illustration of Maintaining the Flow of Instruction as First Response).

Box 5.7	Illustration of Maintaining the Flow of Instruction as First Response

The science teacher was explaining why some volcanoes were extinct and others were not. He directed the class to read the first paragraph of their text on page 84. Steffan, a high-functioning student with ASD, began to mumble and put his head down. The teacher continued, without pausing, to tell the class what to look for in the paragraph. He acknowledged the class for paying attention and approached Steffan, stood beside him for a moment, and said quietly, "Let's get started on the reading, please." Steffan lifted his head and began to read. The teacher said, "Thanks," and moved to another student.

Note: If Steffan had not responded, the teacher—having on a previous occasion seen Steffan withdraw and become very upset when pushed to work—would have permitted him to sit quietly and resume contact in a few minutes. The teacher tried to maintain the flow of instruction as a first response while carefully monitoring Steffan's behavior.

Increase Opportunities to Respond

Simply put, if students are productively engaged in their work, there is less chance of problem behavior. Clearly, if students are required to sit for lengthy periods of time, especially students with problem behavior, without the opportunity to respond or participate, there will be problems. As one teacher remarked, "There is no such thing as dead time for my students. If nothing is going on, they will go into their own routines. Then it is hard to get them back to anything instructional." Similarly, Frase and Hetzel (1990) reported, "The first seven minutes are predictive of how the rest of the lesson will proceed" (pp. 77–78). In addition, especially early in the lesson, students need to have the opportunity to respond *correctly*.

Students with ASD who have social interaction problems often have difficulty knowing how to respond in group work, discussions, and group projects. Given these skill deficiencies, ensure that these students have the opportunity to respond reasonably frequently. In some cases, especially in group project–type activities, these students will probably need some prompts and assistance to participate, otherwise they will be left out of the activity (see Box 5.8: Illustration of Increasing Opportunities to Respond).

Box 5.8	Illustration of Increasing Opportunities to Respond

The science teacher was conducting a class discussion on the flora of the local valley. One student in his class, Cheri, was identified with Asperger syndrome. She was very bright but very unsure of herself when it came to sharing or responding in groups and most often would not initiate any comments. Once the discussion time began, the teacher asked the students to tell their neighbor the name of a flower, shrub, or tree they had seen near the school. He noted that one student was talking to Cheri and Cheri responded. (*Note:* All students, including Cheri, were making a response right at the beginning of class.) The teacher then asked the students to mention to the class what they had just shared. He called on Cheri after a couple of other students had responded. The teacher, in this way, made it fairly easy for Cheri to share with the class by making a response that was already rehearsed with another student. The teacher conducted the rest of the discussion with a mix of sharing with the whole class as well sharing between two students. This structure not only helped Cheri participate but also ensured constant opportunities for all students to respond.

Ensure Fast Pacing

Good pacing is an instructional technique used by teachers to maintain the flow of instruction. Specifically, it is a measure of the *rate* of instructional delivery tied to three areas: (1) the time taken for teachers to present information, (2) the time taken for students to complete a task, and (3) the time between students' completing one task and beginning the next task (Engelmann & Carnine, 1991). There is a solid body of research that links good pacing with high rates of student on-task behavior, and, conversely, slow pacing is correlated with high rates of off-task and disruptive behavior (Darch & Kame'enui, 2004).

Good pacing is absolutely essential when teaching students with ASD. If the pacing is slow, then there is a very high probability that the teacher will lose the students' attention. Once that attention is lost, then the students will resort to their own interests and routines, making it very difficult, if not impossible, for the teacher to regain the students' attention and resume instruction (see Box 5.9: Illustration of Ensuring Fast Pacing).

Box 5.9	Illustration of Ensuring Fast Pacing

The math teacher was presenting information on how to solve a problem. She secured the class's attention and delivered the information in a brisk manner (not rushed, but quickly enough so that the students were able to follow). She told the class that they had 5 minutes to complete the first two problems. After about 5 minutes were up, the teacher secured their attention again, checked whether they were on track with the problem-solving strategy, and then directed them to complete the remaining four problems in their text.

Note: The teacher provided the initial information at a reasonably fast pace, she gave the students sufficient (but not too much) time to complete the task, and there was no down time from when the students finished the task to when the teacher checked their work.

Provide Necessary Prompts

This technique involves providing additional information, such as a hint, cue, or gesture, to a student just prior to engaging the student in a task. Visual cues are particularly helpful prompts for students with ASD. The prompts help the student make the correct response and also help to interrupt a student who may be about to make an incorrect response (Colvin, 2004). This strategy is an effective tool for helping students who are likely to disengage and pursue their own routines. The reason is that the prompt helps the student focus on the expected behavior when difficulties arise (VanDerHeyden, 2005). The key for effective use of prompting is *timing*. Deliver the prompt either prior to the student having an opportunity to make an error or exhibit problem behavior, or at the early onset of the occurrence of an error or problem behavior.

A variation of prompting is known as *advance prompting*. In this case, provide the prompt well ahead of time so that students become aware that change will soon occur. Advance prompts are very useful for helping students make difficult transitions, which is certainly the case for students with ASD (see Box 5.10: Illustration of Providing Necessary Prompting).

Box 5.10	Illustration of Providing Necessary Prompting

Isaac has a hard time with silent reading. Quite often when it is time for reading, he starts to fidget, whine, and self-stimulate. The teacher stands near him and announces to the class, "In a couple of minutes we will be switching over to reading, so please see if you can finish what you are doing," and shows Isaac a visual cue for silent reading—a picture of someone reading (advance prompt). Shortly after, the teacher directs the class to take out their reading books. She approaches Isaac, who is starting to fidget, and holds the visual cue in front of him, saying, "Isaac, let's get started on the reading. You can do it." He grimaces and pulls out a book. The teacher responds, "Great. Thanks."

Shape Responses

Shaping is a common strategy used by teachers, especially for helping students improve the quality of responding when their current level of responding needs improvement. Shaping is the process of successively reinforcing closer approximations of a skill or behavior (Maag, 2004). The strategy is particularly helpful in getting students started on a task that they avoid because of the likelihood of failure when there has been a history of failure with these tasks. Shaping can also help reluctant learners "get over the hump" in surmounting perceived difficulties (see Box 5.11: Illustration of Shaping).

Box 5.11	Illustration of Shaping

Sandra is a high school sophomore and is loosely identified as "high ASD." She received a failing grade for her science class and was vigorously lamenting the result to her resource room teacher. The teacher had established the practice of having Sandra send her a series of emails to problem solve when she was upset about something. Her teacher suggested that Sandra make an appointment to see the science teacher and then directed Sandra to send her an email of what she might say. Here Sandra's first response: "Mr. Hartwig, I am very angry with the grade you gave me for science. I worked hard and deserve better." Her resource room teacher said it is good to let him know she was upset but that she needed to find out how she could get a better grade. Sandra's second response was, "I did not like getting an F and think my project was as good as some of the others who did not get an F." The resource room teacher then said that this put the blame on the teacher and no responsibility on Sandra. Sandra's third message read, "I did not like getting an F and want to talk to you about what I can do to get a better grade." Her resource room teacher said that would do it, and they chatted about some options of what Sandra could do. Sandra then went to visit with her science teacher to discuss her grade and how it could be improved.

The resource room teacher used emails to systematically shape Sandra's thinking in order to prepare her for a productive meeting with her science teacher.

Intersperse Tasks

Some students may get started with an academic task or activity, and when they run into difficulty they quit and then engage in their own routines. This situation often arises with new learning. Task interspersal is a strategy designed to include easier and more reinforcing tasks in the series with harder tasks and has proven to be especially effective with students who have low cognitive skills (Kern & Clemens, 2005). By interspersing easier tasks with more difficult tasks, the student is more likely to be successful and keep working. For example, if the target or difficult task is A, and the easier tasks are B, C, and D, then an interspersal sequence could be: AABCACDAACDAB . . . In this way the student experiences task completion as well as a much higher success rate overall compared to working on the hard examples alone. In general, use previously mastered tasks as the easier tasks that provide the student with the opportunity to practice and maintain mastery of these skills. However, fade out the amount of interspersal tasks once the student is able to work more successfully with the difficult tasks.

The reason is that a review of research shows that the task interspersal strategy may slow down learning (Cates & Dalenberg, 2005). It can also be helpful to combine task interspersal with the behavioral momentum strategy described earlier in this section (see Box 5.12: Illustration of Interspersing Tasks).

Box 5.12	Illustration of Interspersing Tasks

Emily is a first-grade student who has very low communication skills and is learning to name events on her schedule. She can already name certain animals from the picture cards (cat, dog, and horse). The teacher lays out three cards—horse, cat, and snack. Emily is asked to name them with the teacher. Together they say, "Horse, cat, and snack," as the teacher points to each card. The teacher then has Emily name them by herself a couple of times. The teacher then adds the card *choice time,* saying "Choice time." Again Emily is asked to name the cards with the teacher in the order "Horse, snack, cat, choice time." The teacher continues this process of mixing the known cards with the new ones. The mix is gradually adjusted to include more and more of the schedule picture cards and less of the animal cards. In this way Emily was able to be assured of responding correctly a number of times while the new cards were introduced.

Chapter Summary

There are many triggers that set the stage for problem behavior for students with ASD. These triggers include sensory overloading, frustrations with communication and understanding, disruption of routines, surprises and novel situations, undesired activities, setbacks, frustrations with communication and understanding, and skill deficits in many other areas. A student may be functioning reasonably well in the classroom or school activity, but when the triggers become operative, the student begins to have problems, which can lead to meltdowns.

It is most important for teachers and specialists to take every measure possible to identify these triggers and then to implement strategies for preventing the triggers from having negative effects. This chapter describes several strategies for managing triggers, from simple direct measures in the classroom to systematic processes involving comprehensive planning.

The overall assumption in this chapter is that if the triggers are identified and effectively addressed, then the student is much more likely to participate more fully in the classroom activities and less likely to experience problems that may lead to more serious behavior.

6

Agitation Phase

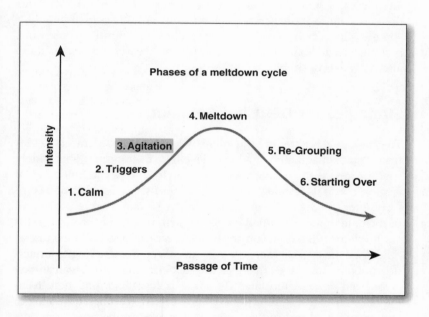

Phases of a meltdown cycle

4. Meltdown

3. Agitation

5. Re-Grouping

2. Triggers

6. Starting Over

1. Calm

Intensity

Passage of Time

S tudents with autism spectrum disorder (ASD) can be having a reasonably successful day in the classroom, especially when teachers and staff consistently implement strategies designed to assist them in the Calm Phase (described in Chapter 4). However, despite these efforts certain triggers come into play that can quickly disrupt the students' calmness and lead to problem behavior. In effect, the students experience a phase change in the meltdown cycle moving to Phase III: Agitation. Here, observable behaviors signal that the students are bothered, upset, worried about something, uneasy, or fearful (behavioral descriptors for this agitated state are presented in Chapter 3). The students have now escalated from the Calm Phase to a higher level of intensity: agitation. In some cases the students will escalate immediately to the Meltdown Phase, skipping the Agitation Phase.

The primary goal in managing behavior in this Agitation Phase is to utilize strategies that are designed to help the students settle down, regain control of themselves, and resume the classroom activities. The alternative, as many teachers have experienced, is that the students may escalate to more serious behavior, specifically a meltdown. Or some students may remain at this level of agitation for some time, making instruction and learning difficult. Clearly, neither of these alternatives is desirable.

Strategies for Defusing Agitation

The basic goal is to reduce the intensity level of the students' behavior from a state of agitation to a lower level—a state of calm. This widely used process is often called *defusion* (Colvin, 2010). The fundamental approach is to use strategies that are supportive, reassuring, and comforting and that are designed to help the students settle down and participate in the scheduled classroom activity.

Implement the defusion strategies *as early as possible* in the phase, otherwise the cycle is more likely to run its course, leading to a meltdown. Sometimes the strategies are ineffective simply because they have been applied too late. The issue is *timing*. Apply these techniques at the earliest indication of agitation. This section describes 16 strategies for addressing agitation that can be applied in classrooms and school settings, which are followed by a checklist and action plan, and procedures for tracking results.

1. Know the Student

While this opening strategy may sound obvious, do all you can to know and understand the individual needs of your students. We noted in Chapter 1 that ASD is a very broad disability category. Consequently, while general strategies may be sound in principle, take steps to make sure the strategies meet the unique needs of these students given the large variability in behavior, skills, and needs. Ensure that specific details are identified about the students, such as their sensory profile; strengths and weaknesses; likes and dislikes; effective modes for communication and understanding; preferred activities; and responsiveness to contact, attention, isolation, and movement. Adopt and adapt aspects of this information in using the remaining strategies for managing agitation. Moreover, share this information with all adults who work in the classroom, with substitute teachers when possible, and with parents as appropriate.

2. Assess Teacher or Adult Response

Another overriding aspect of managing agitation is the way in which the teacher, or other adult, responds to the student who is becoming agitated. Specifically, the demeanor, body language, and bearing of the teacher play a critical role in helping a student who is agitated become settled. Clearly, if the teacher becomes agitated, tense, or annoyed, then the student is likely to become more agitated and perhaps escalate to a meltdown. Conversely, if the teacher is calm, supportive, and reassuring, the student is more likely to become calm or calm down more quickly. Again, it must be stressed that the student's behavior is not directed to the teacher. Rather, it is an over-reaction or an internalized response to triggers they cannot handle.

3. Develop Understanding

A key to helping teachers manage their own behavior when their students become agitated, with the likelihood of a meltdown occurring, is to have a sound understanding of ASD. Understand that the students' behavior usually is not simply willful, oppositional, or manipulative. Rather, a complicated internalization process transpires involving responses to triggers, and the students do not have the necessary resources to manage the agitation that occurs. Essentially, realize that something has triggered the students' behavior that may or may not be identifiable, and that it is very difficult for the students to manage the agitation that follows.

4. Use Empathy

Perhaps the most powerful supportive strategy a teacher may use is to demonstrate empathy. To be effective, empathy involves two critical parts: (1) understanding or recognizing that the student has a problem and (2) communicating concern to the student (Holm, 1997). For example, the teacher may see that the student is using quicker hand movements or beginning to perseverate on certain words (recognition). The teacher then approaches the student and says, "Are you doing OK? Let's see what we are doing here," and joins in the activity the student is currently engaged in (communicates concern). Or the teacher approaches the student and sits near without interaction (to let the student know that teacher is present—physical proximity). It is very important to realize that the strategy of using empathy is much more effective if the teacher has already connected with the student. This connection or relationship has been established by the teacher taking steps to show interest in the student, responding to the student's interests and skills, and giving the student some contact time. In this way, when the student is agitated, he is much more likely to be responsive to the teacher's displays of empathy. By contrast, avoid any communication showing frustration, anxiety, and putting pressure on the student to settle down. This kind of response will more than likely escalate the student. In general, take measures to communicate that you see and understand that the student is having a problem and that you are present with him.

5. Help the Student Focus

Students who display agitation often have difficulty focusing on their work, staying on task, and concentrating. The reason is that they are essentially distracted by whatever it is that is disturbing them. Sometimes the teacher can help the students either get started or resume their work. For example, approach a student who has stopped writing and has begun to tap her pencil on the desk and wave her other arm, and slowly take the pencil, saying, "Here, Ana, let me do the first one. There we go. Now let's see you do the next one." Hand the pencil to Ana, wait for her to continue, and when she starts to write, say, "Nice going, Ana." Sit with her for a few minutes as she begins to write. In this way the student's attention is shifted from the triggers that are bothering her to the specific activities of the lesson. Thus by engaging in the lesson, the student's agitation is often reduced.

6. Provide Space

A very effective strategy for reducing agitation is for the teacher to provide the student with some level of space or isolation from the rest of the class. When students become agitated, they will often seek ways to withdraw from others, such as putting their head down on the desk, refusing to make eye contact or join in discussions, pulling away from the teacher or others when addressed, crawling under a table, or heading to a corner of the room or to a vacant desk. Their message simply is "Leave me alone."

When students seek space, or are given space, two outcomes are likely: (1) they are less likely to be provoked by other people (adults and students) or events and (2) they are provided with an opportunity to settle down, regain focus, and become comfortable enough to resume the class activity.

Common strategies that teachers use to provide space or isolation within the classroom are to establish a quiet area in the room, such as a separate desk or a corner of the room, in order to enable the students to retreat; permit students to put their head down for a while; or allow them to move to an unoccupied desk or table. Sometimes it is helpful to choose a location in the room where there is reduced lighting and to provide the students with headphones. By reducing visual and auditory factors, the teacher provides the student with more chance to calm down. It may be possible to designate some quiet area or space for the student to engage in relaxation activities. Teachers have reported that various kinds of relaxation exercises are helpful in reducing agitation. These activities include the use of audiotapes or CDs, breathing exercises, and relaxation exercises.

Occasionally, it may be appropriate to provide space outside of the classroom for more involved students, such as a supervised place near the office, a corner of another classroom, or a carrel in the library. In these situations arrangements with another staff person must be made ahead of time, and provisions must be made in case the student's behavior escalates. The obvious disadvantage of providing space outside the classroom is that the student is clearly away from instruction and may have difficulty returning to class. Moreover, a staff person has to be taken from the classroom. However, such disadvantages may be necessary in order to avert a meltdown. In general, it is better to provide space within the classroom or the instructional setting.

Again, such strategies may work for some students and may aggravate others. Explore options to find what works best for an individual student.

7. Provide Assurances and Additional Time

In general, students who display agitation on a frequent basis do not have effective problem-solving skills, which, of course, is one of the reasons they become agitated. Problem solving is even more difficult once the students become agitated. They often lack organization skills and the focus necessary to take charge of their responsibilities. Consequently, they may panic and exhibit worse behavior. In these situations give the students some *assurances* and allow more *time* to deal with a task. For example, say something like, "It's OK, Maria. You have plenty of time to complete this" or "Take your time, Marcus. You have 10 minutes yet before the bell rings." In some cases, all the students need is assurance at the onset of agitation. For example, if Tia becomes agitated when she is cleaning up her space, say, "Take your time, Tia. The bus will not leave without you" or "Tia, let me help you so you can get to lunch on time."

8. Permit Special Interest Activities

When students exhibit agitation, they often have difficulty in focusing on a task. It is as if they are seriously distracted. One way of helping them become focused is to permit them to engage in a preferred activity or one of their special interest activities. Because this activity is favored, it is likely to help the students disengage from what is bothering them and become connected with this activity. For example, Charlie, a first-grade student, often has trouble on the bus, so when he enters the classroom he is already upset. Arrange a desk in the corner of the room so that when he enters the room he has the opportunity to immediately play with some Legos. Or there is Luisa, an eighth-grade student who is frequently agitated when she comes to first period, so she is permitted to sit at the back of the room and read some magazines for a few minutes. Similarly, Josh has a hard time walking along the corridors in his high school. He is often subjected to teasing from other students despite teachers' efforts to prevent these occurrences. So when he enters the classroom, he is grumbling over and over about what was said to him. His teacher could arrange a high-interest activity for him, such as time on the computer, so that as soon as he enters the room, he heads to the computer and plays a game for a few minutes.

Set some clear parameters for the student when this strategy is used, otherwise he may not leave the preferred activity or other students may interfere or want to participate. Generally, to offset or precorrect for these problems, rehearse with them the ground rules for engaging in these preferred activities. The rules usually include the following: (1) only one person at a time can engage in the activity or occupy the area; (2) they are to use the activity individually, that is, they are not to invite other students to participate; and (3) they are to engage in the activity for a specified time period, with the expectation that when the time period has elapsed they move promptly to their assigned area or task. For some students it may be desirable to use a timer to communicate how much time they have for the activity and for when the activity is to end.

It is also important to have more than one preferred activity available. The reason is that the student may become tired or bored with the one activity. Take steps to learn which activities the student prefers, either through observation, by talking to the parents, or by talking to the student.

9. Schedule Buffer Breaks

For some students with ASD, or any students for that matter, it is very difficult for teachers to read when they are becoming upset or to pinpoint what triggers upset them. Staff find out too late that the student is upset, and serious problem behavior arises. In these cases, schedule regular breaks to buffer against the student becoming upset. Basically, include breaks as part of the student's regular schedule to provide the opportunity for the student to engage in a preferred activity. So if the student is becoming agitated, but the indicators are not apparent, the break serves to settle the student down and prevent more serious agitation and problem behavior. These breaks are not earned. They are not to be viewed as a privilege for the student. Rather, view them as a necessary part of the student's program based on the student's needs.

10. Use Teacher Proximity

When some students reach the point of agitation, they become insecure and fearful. One reason could be that they have had these experiences before and the outcome has been that they escalate, lose control, and have no way of getting themselves out of the turmoil that arises from a meltdown. Consequently, by standing near the student during this period of agitation, especially early in the phase, the teacher may reassure the student and help the student become less fearful. However, some students will react to the presence of another person by escalating. It is crucial to assess whether or not the student can be approached and how closely you can approach them. Typically, the student's response will provide this information.

Proximity strategies include standing near the student's desk when speaking to the class, making incidental contact with the student, and initiating brief interactions with the student, such as a comment or question such as "How is it going there, Bryan?" or "Looks like you have made a start there, Grace." These contacts should be brief, and if the student reacts a little, usually by body language, withdraw slightly. In this case the student is communicating the need to be left alone. However, reduce the level of proximity just a little before pulling too far away, and watch her responses, because she may want the teacher to be present but not too close.

Do not underestimate the importance of using proximity to assist a student who is agitated. It can be a powerful technique. When the teacher is present to the student during agitation, the student may experience acceptance and support with the overall effect that the student becomes settled.

11. Schedule Independent Activities

One of the simplest strategies for leaving students alone, especially when they are agitated, is to schedule independent activities. Independent work serves several instructional purposes such as opportunities for practice and occasions for mastery and skill assessment. In addition, this simple way of leaving students alone may help them become settled and focused.

One of the most common reasons for students becoming agitated and accelerating their behavior is conflicts or negative interactions with their peers. Independent work helps to factor out interactions between students. In effect, there are fewer distractions, which gives the students more opportunity to focus on the instructional task.

In some cases, there may be several students in the classroom who display agitated behavior on a regular basis. In these cases, schedule independent work activities on a regular basis. Develop the schedule to include some whole-class instruction and small-group activities followed by independent work. Plan to incorporate independent activities on a regular basis throughout the day.

12. Employ Passive Activities

Similarly, following certain events such as recess, gym, or assemblies, the whole class may be overly excited and some students may exhibit agitated behavior (especially students with ASD who may have found the previous activity quite stressful or overstimulating). Utilize passive activities for these kinds of transitions. Passive activities require attention from the students but not much effort in terms of needing to make responses. For example, read a high-interest story to the students; the students are expected to sit quietly and listen. A short video program can serve the same purpose; the students are expected to watch the video and sit quietly. Another example is quietly reading or writing a log if the students have the necessary reading or writing skills. It is also helpful for some students to listen to something with headphones or some combination of headphones and a computer.

13. Use Movement Activities

It is often the case with adults that when they become agitated they begin to move, such as pacing up and down, moving to another area, or getting busy doing something. However, in the classroom students are often expected to sit still, relax, or get on with their work.

Movement is an excellent tool to calm down students who become agitated. Many students automatically show an increase in their behavioral levels when they are agitated. Consequently, when the teacher provides students with an opportunity to move, there is more chance that the students' needs will be met (because they are beginning to move more anyway). The movement activities thereby meet the student needs.

To use this practice effectively, have a ready list of options for movement-oriented activities available, such as running an errand to the office, taking something to a nearby teacher, sorting materials, getting materials ready for another activity, distributing materials, cleaning the board or overheads, going for a walk, shooting hoops, or running around the track with one of the staff. In addition to mitigating agitation, these tasks, or really jobs, set the stage for positive interaction between the teacher and the student.

14. Use Self-Management Approaches When Appropriate

Self-management is the ultimate, long-term goal of any intervention program for problem behavior. Consequently, actively involve students, when the students have the capacity to self-manage, in a plan to control agitation. Students often have their own strategies to reduce agitation and can contribute to the plan or program. For example, Micah had the practice of running away from the classroom when he became upset. So the teacher's arrangement with him was that instead of running away from the classroom, he was permitted to go to a designated area in the school yard. He was given what was called an "energy pass." This practice was adapted for other students as well so that they could initiate a request for an energy pass when they felt they were becoming upset and might have problems. Naturally, these activities need to be supervised and monitored so that they are not overused.

In general there are two steps for involving students in the plan to self-manage agitation: (1) help them identify the onset of their agitation, that is, pinpoint when they first sense they are becoming upset; and (2) arrange a strategy for them to follow when they recognize that they are becoming agitated. For example, Celia, a high-functioning fifth-grade student with Asperger syndrome, begins to shout, grimace, and repeat herself when she becomes agitated. Her teacher sits down with her, shares this observation, and suggests that when she feels upset and thinks she might start shouting, she can go to the quiet area and sit for a while or play with the games there for a few minutes. In this way she is taught to recognize the shouting behavior and to take measures to deal with the situation. Again, if Celia has the skills to debrief, her teacher can sit with her later on to see if it is possible to determine what led to the shouting in the first place and to see if the teacher can develop a plan to address these triggers.

15. Establish Relaxation Centers

Sometimes teachers take steps to add relaxation centers to their classroom, which have the effect of calming or relaxing their students. For example, place certain furniture in the corner of a room, such as a large beanbag or a rocking chair. The beanbag serves students who are helped by being still, while the rocking chair serves students who need to move. It is quite common to see a small aquarium in a classroom. Many times students can be calmed by rhythmic sounds or movement. Some students may relax by listening to soothing sounds. Others may be helped by watching the rhythmic and constant motion of a mobile, a spinning top, or circling fish in a classroom aquarium. Place the aquarium in a quiet area of the room to help the students calm down. In addition, benefits can be obtained by involving students in taking care of the aquarium (feeding the fish, cleaning the unit). Again, the benefits of an aquarium must be weighed against the time needed to maintain it over the holidays and weekends. Finally, the students who have proprioceptive and vestibular issues may be calmed down by having access to a rocking chair, bouncing ball, or mini trampoline.

16. Provide Physical Contact as Appropriate

Some students can receive relief and comfort through physical contact in which pressure is applied, such as in a tight squeeze, being held in a hug, or being rocked. This approach is quite common with young children. Rhythmic rocking, accompanied with quiet talk, can have a very soothing effect, reduce agitation, and prevent escalation.

Keep in mind that some students will react negatively to being touched and certainly to being held. Watch the students carefully to observe their response to physical contact for feedback on whether the approach is helpful or not.

It is very important to understand that we are not talking about physical restraint here; this topic will be carefully addressed in Chapter 7 on managing meltdowns. Rather, the physical contact here is meant to be gentle and soothing, designed to be used early in the cycle, at the Agitation Phase, rather than designed to prevent behavior that could result in children hurting themselves or others that may occur later in the cycle, the Meltdown Phase.

In general, use physical contact as a useful strategy for young children, and be sure to have parental approval for how you use it so that it is not confused with restraint.

Checklist and Action Plan

Given that there is an extensive range of needs for students with ASD and several strategies for defusing agitation, we strongly recommend that teachers take time to plan in sufficient detail how to address their students' agitation behavior. See Form 6.1: Illustration of a Checklist and Action Plan for Defusing Agitation, which correlates with the 16 strategies described above. A blank version of this checklist and action plan is included in Appendix H. We also recommend that this action plan be reviewed and updated periodically.

Form 6.1   Illustration of Checklist and Action Plan for Defusing Agitation

Strategy	Action
1. Know the student	Carefully review all assessment material and address gaps as needed.
2. Assess teacher or adult response	Monitor.
3. Develop understanding	Read literature where possible and attend professional development opportunities.
4. Use empathy	Be aware of reactions and how you are communicating support.
5. Help the student focus	Use direct language and visual supports.
6. Provide space	Check desk area.
7. Provide assurances and additional time	Take steps to reduce pressure.
8. Permit special interest activities	Identify special interests. Develop menu.
9. Schedule buffer breaks	Schedule two additional breaks.
10. Use teacher proximity	Check student's response to teacher proximity and use accordingly.
11. Schedule independent activities	Schedule independent work during and at the end of instructional periods.
12. Employ passive activities	Use reading to class for 5 minutes after recess.
13. Use movement activities	Use student as assistant in handing out class material.
14. Use self-management approaches when appropriate	Teach student to check work completion.
15. Establish relaxation centers	Use rocking chair for buffer breaks.
16. Provide physical contact as appropriate	Check with family and previous teachers on use of this strategy.

Tracking Results

It is particularly important to track results so that if the students are not making gains or maintaining improvement, then intervention adjustments can be made in a timely manner. The most useful measures relate to the meltdowns that are the primary focus of this book. The major thrust of using strategies to defuse agitation is to prevent escalation leading to meltdowns. The critical measures regarding meltdowns are *frequency* (how often the meltdowns occur), *duration* (how long the meltdowns last), and *intensity* (how serious, disruptive, or unsafe the behavior is). Clearly, reduction in frequency, duration, and intensity of meltdowns is the goal of interventions used during Phases I–III. When reductions occur, teachers and specialists can conclude that the strategies used are effective and should be maintained. However, when reductions in meltdowns do not occur, then several conclusions can be reached that need to be carefully examined by the teachers and specialists. Possible explanations are that the strategies used

1. Need to be adjusted or replaced.

2. Are not being implemented consistently.

3. Need to be implemented over a longer time before results will be obtained.

4. Are being implemented too late. The issue is timing. The key is to implement the strategies at the very earliest indication of agitation.

5. Are not appropriate because other triggers are operating that have not been identified and would require different strategies.

Note: In some cases there are interactions between frequency, duration, and intensity of meltdowns. That is, the duration of the meltdowns may decrease, but the frequency may increase. This situation is relatively common. The reduction in duration needs to be interpreted as a *positive* result even with accompanying increases in frequency. The reason is that some students go through a gradual process of taking control of meltdowns. It is very difficult to really know what is going on for some students. However, the rule is that if there is a reduction in duration or intensity, then progress is being made. More detail is provided on these measures in Chapter 7.

By systematically tracking the occurrence of meltdowns (frequency, duration, and intensity), teachers and specialists are in a position to make judgments and decisions on the strategies being used to defuse agitation and prevent meltdowns.

Chapter Summary

Managing agitation is a critical step in the overall plan for preventing meltdown behavior in students with ASD. If teachers can successfully defuse the agitation, the students will become settled and resume the classroom activities more fully, thereby preempting more serious meltdown behavior. Moreover, when students are agitated, they have difficulty engaging in their schoolwork. Basically, they are distracted, so when they become more settled, they become more engaged in instruction and learning is more likely to occur.

This chapter describes 16 strategies to defuse agitation. However, given the wide range of ability levels and needs of students with ASD, there is no telling which strategies may be more or less effective with any given student. Some strategies that help certain students may exacerbate the problems for other students. Which strategy will work will be determined by each student's response. In general, try different strategies, and carefully observe the effects on student behavior to determine which strategies are more effective for the students.

An overall guideline in using these strategies is to implement them at the earliest possible signs of agitation. The more a student becomes agitated, the more difficult it will be to defuse the situation.

It is also very important to track the occurrences of meltdowns (frequency, duration, and intensity) so that the effectiveness of the defusion strategies can be determined and timely adjustments made as needed.

The key assumption underlying the implementation of these strategies is that students need help and support to manage agitation. Typically, students with ASD are deficient in the personal resources or skills needed to manage the triggers that set off their problem behavior. By understanding this central dimension of the disability of ASD, teachers will be in a stronger position to determine the level of support needed to be effective with these high-needs students.

7

Meltdown Phase

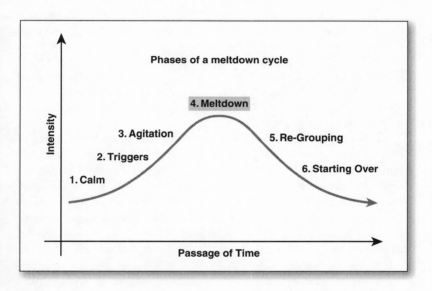

Phases of a meltdown cycle

Intensity

4. Meltdown

3. Agitation

2. Triggers

1. Calm

5. Re-Grouping

6. Starting Over

Passage of Time

Even though teachers, staff, and parents may have worked very assiduously to keep the student in the early phases of the meltdown cycle by maximizing instruction, encouraging student engagement, and establishing good communication systems (Phase I); pinpointing several triggers and taking systematic steps to address them (Phase II); and catching early signs of agitation and using defusion strategies (Phase III), *meltdowns still occur.* The reality is that the field still has a lot to learn about autism spectrum disorder (ASD) in general, and the causes and processes of meltdowns in particular. However, we do know that they can be reduced and that there are helpful practices and procedures for managing meltdowns when they occur.

Students typically reach the Meltdown Phase through two paths (noted in Chapter 2). First, there are students who reach this phase in stages. They begin in the Calm Phase, then triggers come into play, which have the effect of increasing the intensity level of the students' behavior, leading to the Agitation Phase. Triggers may continue to operate, or additional triggers may emerge, which bring about a meltdown. The second path followed by some students, as noted in Chapter 6, bypasses the Agitation Phase and goes straight to a meltdown. They are in the Calm Phase, triggers surface, and the students accelerate immediately to the Meltdown Phase (sometimes called *catastrophic reaction;* Grandin, 2011). In either case, the students reach the Meltdown Phase—the highest, most intense, and most worrisome level of behavior in the cycle.

This chapter describes best practice and research-based strategies for managing meltdowns. It cannot be overstated that dealing directly with meltdowns when they occur is but one component in the six-phase meltdown cycle. While it is critical to be as fully versed as possible in effectively addressing this phase, there are five other phases that play a significant role in the prevention and management of meltdowns. *All phases* in the cycle must be effectively dealt with for meltdowns to be prevented in the first place and efficiently managed when they do occur.

There are three major sections in this chapter that are central to the proper management of meltdowns: (1) critical perspectives, (2) essential prerequisite steps, and (3) intervention steps.

Critical Perspectives

Given that meltdowns represent the most intense level of behavior in the cycle, at which point safety and disruption are of serious concern, several key perspectives need to be understood before the strategies are implemented. These foundations describe the main ideas behind the strategies, thereby enabling teachers, support staff, and parents to effectively use the tools and make adaptations as necessary.

Putting Safety First

The most crucial rule in developing procedures for managing meltdowns is *safety first*. Sometimes there are tradeoffs between what is best practice regarding reinforcement principles and safety. For example, it may be better to ignore or delay responding to certain behaviors because providing attention will reinforce them. However, if someone is likely to get hurt, then staff must respond swiftly and effectively to ensure the safety of the involved student or the other students, regardless of whether attention is being provided to the problem behavior. The basic rule in the overall program is *safety first*.

Understanding That Meltdowns Will Run Their Course

First and foremost, teachers, support persons, and parents have to understand that there is a certain powerlessness in their ability to intervene and stop a meltdown. Many of us have had some experience with other children who become very upset over something, whether it arises from pain, discomfort, or some significant setback for them. In these cases it is usually possible to comfort the child, provide assurances, distract the child, talk to him or her, problem solve, and in direct ways alleviate the problem. However, this is not the case regarding meltdowns with children who have ASD. In fact, many of these direct kinds of interventions will more than likely exacerbate the situation, prolong the meltdown, cause more disruption, and in some cases cause injuries either to the student or others.

There is a very important rule to remember: *A meltdown will typically run its course*. Clearly, there are steps staff can take, and must take, but the bottom line is that direct interventions will not disrupt a meltdown. There are strategies that can help a student slowly gain control, but there are no *quick fixes* to quickly break up a meltdown. The process is typically *very slow* for students to gain control during and following a meltdown. This understanding will help to define the role and disposition of staff when meltdowns occur.

Understanding That Meltdowns Are Not Tantrums

One of the most challenging aspects for teachers and specialists dealing with meltdowns is the question of providing support. The issue is that staff may believe they are reinforcing the very problem behavior they are trying to change when they are being supportive during a meltdown. For example, a teacher is encouraged to be present and supportive to a student during a meltdown. However, this teacher has been quite successful in working with students who display serious acting-out behavior and tantrums and has learned to monitor the students but to keep a distance and maintain an aloof presence. Otherwise, there is the risk that the whole chain of behavior may be reinforced when it comes to managing tantrums.

The position taken in this book is that meltdowns are a *different kind of response class* from acting-out behavior and tantrums. The assumption is that meltdowns are driven by internalized processes in reaction to sensory overloading, cognitive dysfunctions, and socialization problems (described in Chapters 2 and 5). The students do not have sufficient internal resources to manage these reactions, so their behavior is driven by fear or panic. Their behavior is fundamentally reactive to processes they cannot control. The interventions for the Meltdown Phase are designed to provide support to allay the fear and panic and enable the students to eventually take control of themselves. In contrast, tantrums and acting-out behavior are viewed as fundamentally manipulative and driven by some unmet need in the environment. The students want something, or want to avoid something, and have not been successful. If teachers provide what they want, then the tantrum is successful. Interventions for this behavior are designed to settle down the students and then to teach other ways, besides tantrums, to obtain what they need (Colvin, 2004).

Simply put, with meltdowns students are centered on *internal* reactions—their fears, confusion, and anxieties—whereas with tantrums students are centered on taking control of the environment, *external* reactions—getting what they want or avoiding what they do not want. In other words, a student in a meltdown is seeking relief from excessive reactions to certain triggers. Whereas a student in a tantrum wants to get his own way in obtaining something or avoiding something. It is important to clarify this distinction in delivering interventions for effectively managing either meltdowns or tantrums.

Using Restraint Judiciously

Restraint has been a common strategy used by staff over the years to manage students who have meltdowns and acting-out behavior incidents. Today, the field is very much aware of the problems that inappropriate use of restraint has caused in terms of injury—and tragically, in some cases, death—to these students. Also, people have been ill advised to hold the students when they are in a meltdown on the basis that students need the security provided by being held. However, in the heightened situation of a meltdown, serious injuries have occurred when force is used to hold students. So what is a reasonable response to an educator who asks, "So is restraint an option?" or "When can you use restraint?" Our position is that there is no single correct answer to these questions. Restraint can be part of a continuum of interventions; it should only be used as a *last resort* when someone is in danger of being injured and should never be used as an intervention to disrupt a meltdown. The practices used, or intended to be used, must be approved by the district and parents and must be reflected in the student's Individual Education Plan (IEP). Moreover, there need to be clear-cut guidelines in how and when restraint is to be used. The following general guidelines are summarized from our research into current practices in school districts:

1. All staff need to be fully trained in knowing the very limited circumstances in which restraint may be appropriate.

2. Staff need to be fully trained in all aspects of managing meltdowns before restraint is even considered.

3. Safe rooms need to be readily available and procedures in place to speedily relocate other students if need be.

4. No physical responses from staff should occur as a first response to a meltdown. The meltdown should be allowed to run its course. Screaming and yelling with high intensity, running around, and thrashing on the floor are not dangerous situations if a safe room has been established. The meltdown should just run its course, with standard supportive behaviors provided by staff.

5. If injury is occurring, or likely to occur, such as the students banging their head on the wall, pulling their hair, hitting or scratching their face, or attempting to do such to others—*safe restraint procedures may be used.* Safe restraint is a generic approach to preventing injury from aggressive acts; it is essentially *passive.* That is, the student is prevented from hurting herself or others by steering the student away or blocking her arms or hands. For example, a student may be trying to hit her head, so the adult puts his or her arm between the student's arm and head. Note the student's arm is not held and is free to move, but cannot move to hit her head. It is beyond the scope of this book to provide details for safe restraint training.

However, there are professionally approved programs that offer training. Box 7.1: Resources for Safe Restraint Training provides some critical information on the use of restraint and safe restraint training programs.

Box 7.1	Resources for Safe Restraint Training

Critical Information on Use of Restraint

National Disability Rights Network. (2009). *School Is Not Supposed to Hurt: Update on Progress in 2009 to Prevent and Reduce Restraint and Seclusion in Schools.* Washington, DC: National Disability Rights Network.

Ryan, J. B., & Peterson, R. (2004). Physical Restraint in Schools. *Behavioral Disorders, 29,* 154–168.

U.S. Department of Education. (2010). *Summary of Seclusion and Restraint Statutes, Regulations, Policies and Guidance, by State and Territory: Information as Reported to the Regional Comprehensive Centers and Gathered from Other Sources.* Washington, DC: Author.

Products and Training Programs

Nonviolent Crisis Intervention Training: www.crisisprevention.com/Special ties/Nonviolent-Crisis-Intervention

NAPPI (Non Abusive Psychological and Physical Intervention) Resource Center: www.nappi-training.com/category/4956/nappi-resource-center.htm

Handle With Care: Behavior Management System: http://handlewithcare .com/contact

6. Complete documentation must be taken. Usually an incident report or standard form is completed. A sample incident report form (Form 7.1) is presented later in this chapter.

7. A follow-up meeting should be held as soon as possible following a meltdown for which restraint has been used. The purpose of the meeting is to review the whole meltdown cycle in order to determine what changes could be made to avoid using restraint in future occurrences of meltdowns.

In general, there are a number of steps that need to be in place before any form of restraint is used. If restraint has to be used, approval by the district and parents must be in place beforehand, and any persons using restraint need to be trained in *safe restraint* procedures and rigidly follow the district's policy and procedures for using restraint.

Essential Prerequisite Steps

Again, given the serious nature of meltdowns, a number of steps must be firmly in place beforehand. The prerequisite steps for managing meltdowns are analogous to crisis and emergency procedures followed in schools. The procedures need to be carefully thought through, laid out, readily available, and fully disseminated with appropriate training for all faculty members likely to be involved. These prerequisite steps, when properly addressed, will make it easier and smoother for all concerned to implement the strategies more effectively when meltdowns occur. If these steps are not in place, there is much more likelihood of someone getting hurt, significant disruption occurring, and the meltdowns continuing at the same or more intense levels. This section describes six prerequisites steps for addressing meltdowns that can be applied in classrooms and other school settings. We recommend that a checklist be used to ensure that these prerequisite steps are adequately addressed. A sample checklist and action form with an illustration is provided at the end of this section.

Step 1: Obtain Parent Approval

Ideally, students with ASD, especially those who exhibit meltdowns, have an IEP that includes details for managing the meltdowns. It is absolutely essential for parents and guardians to be fully informed and, ideally, active participants in the development of the procedures. It is most important to obtain parent approval and input for measures taken to manage meltdowns.

Step 2: Arrange Professional Preparation for Staff

Ensure that all staff members who have any direct responsibilities, such as providing instruction, assistance, and supervision, receive adequate training in safe and effective strategies for managing meltdowns for students with ASD. If this training does not occur, staff will typically follow their own instincts, which may escalate the situation even further.

Similarly, ensure that adequate training is also provided to substitute teachers and assistants who work in the classroom. If substitute teachers or assistants are not trained in the procedures, then designate staff in the classroom or building to take charge should a meltdown occur.

Step 3: Arrange Preparation for Office Staff and Administration

School administrators and office staff need to be fully informed of what to expect and what their role may be when meltdowns occur. The intensity and duration of a meltdown can be quite disconcerting to administrators, office staff, and other teachers for that matter, if they are not adequately informed, and they may take action that is counterproductive.

Step 4: Follow School Policies and the IEP

It is standard practice for schools to have quite clear-cut policies and procedures for school safety and emergency procedures for students who may exhibit serious acting-out and unsafe behavior. These policies and procedures are designed to serve all students. However, in responding to meltdowns for students with ASD, it is absolutely essential for teachers and administrators to follow the individualized procedures that have been arranged for these students, usually in the IEP. This may mean that an exception is made to the schoolwide procedures. For example, it may be an option for the administration to call the police for certain out-of-control, aggressive, and unsafe behavior or to suspend students for these behaviors. However, for a student with ASD in a full-scale meltdown, the plan may be to remove other students from the classroom or area, closely monitor the student until he calms down, and resume the classroom activities. Police would not be called, nor would the student be suspended.

It is most important that the administration and faculty understand that different procedures, or exceptions, must be applied for students with ASD who are experiencing meltdowns. If these understandings are not present, then students with ASD may have their rights breached, causing serious problems for the individual students and probable liabilities for the school.

Step 5: Ensure Classroom and Schoolwide Readiness

Define Roles. Teachers responsible for the education of students with ASD have a solid plan in place beforehand so that if a meltdown should occur, then everyone in the classroom knows exactly what his or her role is. There is no place for calling a quick meeting to determine what to do or responding in an impulsive or instinctual manner. All should know what to do. Granted, adjustments may need to be made if unforeseen events arise. But the bottom line is that there is a plan in place and everyone knows what to do.

Establish Flexibility. The plan usually calls for flexibility. For example, if the meltdown occurs at the end of the day, then it is usually not appropriate to put the involved student on the bus while the meltdown is occurring. Arrange alternative transportation beforehand. Similarly, it may be time for lunch for the staff person who is monitoring the student involved in a meltdown; schedule adjustments need to be made so that the monitoring is not interrupted.

Explain Documentation Needs. Careful documentation must be a key part of the plan. Write up and file information related to the meltdown so that parents are given adequate information on the incident, decisions can be made for adjusting the plan as necessary, aspects of triggers may be identified, details of the student responses are described, and fidelity to the plan is noted. Provide adequate training for staff in what documentation is needed and the process to follow.

Provide Staff Support. Taking charge of a meltdown can be very draining for staff, especially when sustained screaming and physical excesses are involved, such as kicking, flailing of arms, and banging on walls. Develop a plan so that staff members responsible for monitoring and managing the meltdown have a short break following the meltdown to collect themselves before working with other students or the same student.

Minimize Classroom Disruption. Given that other students are in class and involved with instruction, the procedures for managing meltdowns must be designed to minimize disruption for the rest of the class. The procedures must not only be safe for the involved student but also enable instruction to continue for the rest of the class as much as possible. Typically, the student experiencing the meltdown is separated from the rest of the class by moving the class to another nearby setting or carefully guiding the involved student to a separate room or location.

Step 6: Prepare the Students

Inform both the individual student and the whole class of the procedures. Typically, you would take the individual student aside and carefully explain the details of the plan. Adjust the amount of detail and level of explanation according to the student's level of functioning or capacity to understand the explanations. Conduct this review time when the student is calm to maximize understanding and cooperation. Also, rehearse or practice the procedures with younger students to assist understanding.

Carefully rehearse the expectations with the whole class regarding the classroom practices used to help students who are having behavioral problems. Thoroughly explain the classroom management system to the students so that when the occasion warrants intervention, there will be no surprises or confusion for the students.

Students who are not involved with the incident need to understand what is expected of them and how they can help each other. Specifically, other students need to follow the teacher's directions quickly, stay focused on the classroom activity, and especially avoid any involvement with the incident. Also, at times they may need to be asked to cooperate with a *room clear*, gather their materials quickly, and move to the designated location. Basically, the planning and practice needs to be presented to the class as an *emergency*, and full cooperation is expected.

Moreover, if a meltdown occurs at a later date and the teacher believes there was considerable confusion or delays in responding by the class, the involved students, or other staff for that matter, additional explanations and practice need to be offered in order to ensure smoother responses in the future.

Checklist and Action Plan

Form 7.1: Illustrations of Checklist and Action Plan for Prerequisite Steps in Managing Meltdowns is a helpful guide to use in this phase. A blank version is included in Appendix I.

Form 7.1 Illustration of Checklist and Action Plan for Prerequisite Steps in Managing Meltdowns

Student Level: Junior high school student placed in resource room, mild intellectual disabilities, verbal, can follow written schedule, highly distractible and displays impulsive behavior.

Step	Date	Action
Step 1: Obtain parent approval	10/12/11	Schedule meeting with parents, involved staff, and administrator.
Step 2: Arrange professional preparation for staff	10/28/11	Schedule all involved staff for afterschool training session to explain and model details of the intervention plan. Invite parents as appropriate.
Step 3: Arrange preparation for office staff and administration	11/1/11	Meet with office staff and administration to explain and clarify support roles.
Step 4: Follow school policies and the IEP	Ongoing	Ensure that discrepancies between school policies for all students and details on the student's IEP are clarified and any issues resolved.
Step 5: Ensure classroom and schoolwide readiness	Ongoing	a. Define roles. b. Establish flexibility. c. Explain documentation needs. d. Provide staff support. e. Minimize classroom disruption.
Step 6: Prepare the students	11/3/11	a. Walk student through procedures. b. Address whole class on emergency procedures, emphasizing their responsibilities.

Intervention Steps

It has been well established that students with ASD exhibit a very wide range of needs and respond to interventions in highly individualized ways, especially when it comes to developing and implementing plans to address meltdowns. The following strategies are described as a source for the details of a plan. There is no guarantee that the strategies will be effective for each student. Rather, the recommendation is to draw on these strategies, individually or in combination, to develop a plan for individual students. It is expected that the plan will be adapted over time as the student progresses or does not progress satisfactorily. The overall plan for managing a meltdown typically involves five steps in helping the student recover from a meltdown. This section describes these steps and presents a sample checklist and action form with an illustration.

Step 1: Guide the Student to the Safe Place

The most important first step in managing meltdowns is to have a safe place where the student can move to at the onset of a meltdown. Ideally, this safe place is a small room attached to or very close to the classroom. The room is called safe for two reasons. It is a room where the student knows she is safe and that the meltdown can run its course. Second, objects are removed from this room that could be used to cause injury (extra chairs, pencils, pens, any sharp objects, and equipment). The space should be basically empty except for some cushions or beanbags and a chair for the adult monitoring and providing support to the students. Beforehand, when the student is calm, be sure to carefully rehearse with her how to go to the safe place. This is much like practicing fire drills to prepare ahead of time for the event of an actual fire.

Take great care in how the student gets to the safe place. Do not physically force the student. Physical force in this situation invariably escalates the student further and sets the occasion for someone to get hurt. Patiently guide the student to the area, and avoid any communication of anxiety or urgency to get the student there.

Have a set phrase for going to the safe place, such as "(Student's first name), let's move to the safe place" (rehearse this phrase with the student beforehand). Take a step toward the safe room, point to the room, and repeat the phrase "safe place." Also use a picture if visual supports are commonly used with the student.

If the student is having difficulty in getting to the safe space and is seriously disrupting the classroom, conduct a *room clear* in which the other students in the class are directed to move to a designated classroom or area, leaving the involved student with an adult (Colvin, 2004). Rehearse the room clear procedure with the class so that students and staff can respond very quickly, quietly, and, ideally, automatically. Once the involved student permits herself to be guided to the safe area, other students can be given the signal to return to class at the most convenient opportunity.

Step 2: Implement Supportive Measures

How teachers or adults play their role in monitoring and dealing with the meltdown is absolutely crucial in helping the student settle down. The basic approach involves understanding that they cannot stop and disrupt the meltdown much as they would like to—the meltdown will run its course. However, there are certain *supportive* teacher behaviors that, in time, will help the student settle down and assist with his recovery. By contrast, certain teacher behaviors should be studiously avoided that are highly likely to escalate the student, prolong the meltdown, and make transition more difficult. Examples of each type are presented in Box 7.2: Supportive and Unsupportive Practices During Student Meltdowns.

Box 7.2	Supportive and Unsupportive Practices During Student Meltdowns

Supportive Practices *Should Do*	*Unsupportive Practices* *Should Not Do*
Maintain a calm, positive presence.	Display agitated, negative presence.
Communicate understanding that the meltdown will take its time.	Communicate that the meltdown must stop immediately.
Realize reasoning will not help. Restrict comments to supportive statements.	Try to reason, talk the student through it, and ask lots of questions.
Lower voice and slow down speech.	Raise voice and speak rapidly.
Remain present, but give the student space.	Crowd the student.

(Continued)

(Continued)

Supportive Practices Should Do	Unsupportive Practices Should Not Do
Assume a relaxed posture.	Assume an assertive posture.
Slow down movements, and be still.	Hasten movements, communicating urgency.
Communicate patience in that the student has permission for the meltdown to run its course.	Use threats or warnings: "If this does not stop, you will miss the next break."
Talk calmly and encouragingly.	Talk firmly and seriously to the student.
Avoid physical contact.	Use physical contact (hold the student's arm, or hold the student down).
Communicate empathy that the student is having a rough time.	Communicate that the behavior is unacceptable.
Show encouragement when the student begins to settle: "Good. I am happy you are feeling better."	Show annoyance that it took so long settle: "Yes. It's time you settled down."

The basic approach in this step is to patiently ride out the meltdown in a safe place, provide support, and look for signs that the intensity of the meltdown may be decreasing. Then, and only then, move to Step 4 (Identify Signs of Meltdown Recovery).

Step 3: Manage More Than One Meltdown at a Time (as Needed)

Teachers often complain, and rightly so, that information and training for them is usually geared to dealing with just one student who is having serious problems. However, it is very common in schools to place students with ASD and other students who have problem behavior in one classroom. Consequently, when one student has a meltdown, other students may be triggered so that multiple meltdowns occur at the same time. The question becomes this: What do you do if more than one meltdown is happening at the same time?

As with the case of a single meltdown, preparation is the key. Students who are likely to have meltdowns are usually placed in classrooms with both a teacher and support staff, typically teacher assistants, all of whom should be provided with adequate training in procedures for managing multiple meltdowns. The standard procedure is to separate the students. Call a room clear for the noninvolved students. If two students are having a meltdown, guide one to a safe area and the other to another designated location that is also safe. If more meltdowns are occurring, or there are difficulties in guiding the students to the safe areas, make a request for assistance. Procedures for making a *request for assistance* should already have been established beforehand. The request for assistance could to be to the front office, where there is a list of people designated to respond, such as an administrator, security personnel, a behavior specialist, or support staff (counselor, school psychologist, or social worker).

The key in calling for assistance is the ready availability of someone to help and that this person is trained and knows exactly how to help. Again, this list of personnel needs to be readily accessible (usually by connecting through the front office). In summary, a system needs to be in place: a staff person who makes the call (usually the teacher or designated assistant), an initial contact person (typically in the front office), a list of possible responders, and all persons on the list are clear on what is expected of them.

Finally, if multiple meltdowns occur frequently in the classroom, it may be necessary to conduct an evaluation of the classroom procedures, the adequacy of staffing in the classroom, and placement options for the involved students.

Step 4: Identify Signs of Meltdown Recovery

While there is considerable variability in how long a meltdown will last, there is the common factor that it will end at some point. However, a meltdown typically does not end abruptly. Students exiting a meltdown generally do so in gradual stages or degrees. There are usually one or two signs that a student may be exiting a meltdown:

1. There is a noticeable *decrease in intensity* in the student's behavior, such as a reduction in volume of the screaming and yelling, less physical intensity of body movements (thrashing on the

floor, arm waving or flapping, and running around the room), less physical tension in the body, or a switch from loud perseverative talk to mumbling.

2. The student becomes *more tuned into the environment,* such as by looking at the adult, attending to items in the room, responding to supportive comments from the adult, or asking questions or making comments directed to the adult.

At this juncture begin to take the steps for exiting the meltdown and beginning the next phase (Re-Grouping, discussed in Chapter 8).

Step 5: Document the Meltdown Incident

Document the meltdown incident as fully as possible. Note details in the report to provide information on what is reported to the parents, used for determination of IEP progress, and for modifying the management plan as needed. Use a set form for writing up the incident. The form will help teachers and staff in being consistent with what they write down and also ensure that complete information is recorded. Information reported typically includes the following details, which are followed by Form 7.2: Incident Report for a Meltdown (which can also be found in Appendix J).

- Demographic information on the student (name, class, teacher, date)
- Name of the person writing report
- Any injuries sustained by the student, other students, or staff
- Start time and end time of the meltdown (duration of the meltdown)
- Classroom activity at onset of the meltdown
- Name of the staff member initially involved with the student
- Name of the staff member mostly involved with managing the meltdown
- Initial steps taken by the teacher or staff
- Possible initial triggers
- Signs of agitation preceding the meltdown, if present
- Specific behaviors exhibited by the student during the meltdown
- Transition stages from meltdown to recovery
- Responses by staff during the meltdown
- Additional steps taken (parent contact, meeting called, other)

Form 7.2   Incident Report for a Meltdown

Student Name _____ Grade _____ Date _____

Written by _____ Classroom teacher _____

Staff member initially involved _____

Staff member managing incident _____

Start time of incident _____ End time _____ Duration _____

Report of any injuries sustained: _____
_____

Initial steps taken by staff member: _____
_____

List of possible triggers: _____
_____

List of agitation signs: _____
_____

Behaviors during meltdown: _____
_____

Responses by staff member during meltdown: _____
_____

Transition stages from meltdown to recovery: _____
_____

Additional steps taken:

Parent contact _____ Meeting called _____ Other _____

Checklist and Action Plan

Form 7.3: Illustration of Checklist and Action Plan for Intervention Steps in Managing a Meltdown is another helpful resource in the process of managing meltdowns. A blank version is included in Appendix K.

Form 7.3 Illustration of Checklist and Action Plan for Intervention Steps in Managing a Meltdown

Student Level: High functioning, verbal, literal, with Asperger syndrome, in general education classes for most subjects with support.

Step	Action
Step 1: Guide the student to the safe place	*General education teacher makes call to administrator, who responds quickly and quietly and privately requests that student follow her. Administrator takes student to vacant room adjacent to office (this location and practice has been predetermined).*
Step 2: Implement supportive measures	*Administrator, trained and practiced in supportive procedures, calmly prompts student to take a seat and take a few deep breaths and wait. Administrator withdraws and stands near door in detached and nonthreatening manner.*
Step 3: Manage more than one meltdown at a time (as needed)	*Not applicable*
Step 4: Identify signs of meltdown recovery	*Student begins to look around, breathing more evenly, and sits quietly. Administrator calls student by name, and student looks across. Administrator says, "Great, I am glad you are doing better."*
Step 5: Document the meltdown incident	*Administrator completes incident report (Form 7.1).*

Chapter Summary

The very mention of the word *meltdown* brings a definite feeling of tension and concern to teachers and support personnel when it comes to teaching students with ASD. Meltdowns have significant impact in a classroom and can lead to immediate disruption and unsafe situations. For these reasons the management procedures for this phase of the cycle must be clearly prescribed, and all staff members involved with the students must receive adequate training. The procedures have three clear emphases: First, perspectives related to the nature of meltdowns need to be understood. Second, a number of prerequisite conditions must be in place, centering on setup details and training needs for all involved staff. Finally, in the event that a meltdown occurs, everyone needs to know the actual intervention steps teachers and support staff can use to manage the meltdown in a safe and supportive way that can ultimately lead to the student's recovery. Careful and complete documentation must be completed to notify parents and guardians of the incident and to provide a basis for follow-up, especially in terms of adjustments that may need to be made to the intervention procedures.

8

Re-Grouping Phase

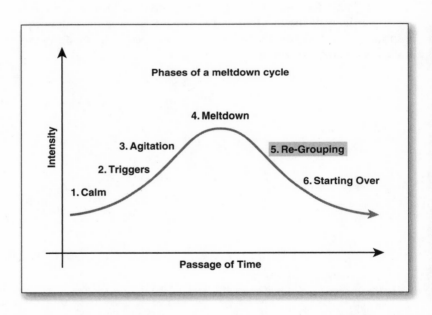

The fifth phase in the model for the meltdown cycle provides a series of steps to help students with autism spectrum disorder (ASD) transition from a meltdown to activities in the regular schedule. This transition phase is called Phase V: Re-Grouping.

When a student is engaged in a meltdown with sustained disruption, loud, sometimes deafening screaming, and displays of physical excesses with legs flailing on the floor and arms flapping intensively, the period may seem interminable for the staff involved. However, the student's behavior will eventually subside either as a result of the supportive strategies used by staff or simply as a function of exhaustion. The period immediately following a meltdown is called *re-grouping*, or sometimes reintegration. The students are essentially in a transition process of resuming their normal emotional and intellectual functioning following an episode of a meltdown when they have not been able to regulate their emotions or cognitive functions.

The following steps are designed, in sequence, to systematically manage this transition from meltdown to recovery: (1) critical perspectives, (2) behavioral indicators that the meltdown is ending, and (c) intervention steps.

Critical Perspectives

Just as in the case of managing meltdowns, there are certain key perspectives for the supervising adult to clearly understand when it comes to helping a student through this Re-Grouping Phase. If the perspectives are understood and put into practice, then there is much more chance of a successful transition to recovery. If not, the transition period may likely take longer and there is every chance the student may return to the Meltdown Phase.

The Transition Is an Incremental Process

It is imperative to realize that the transition from a meltdown to a recovery occurs in degrees. Generally, there is no such thing as a quick jump to normalcy for the student following a meltdown. Rather, the process is marked with discrete and observable changes, from out-of-control behavior to regular functioning. These stages need to be recognized and responded to for a relatively smooth transition to occur.

The Transition Will Run Its Course

Do not be trapped into watching the clock to see how long the recovery is taking, thinking that the student may have had enough time to recover. This is a serious mistake and may likely lead to a recurrence of a meltdown if you assume that the student has had enough time and try to accelerate the process. Similarly, the schedule may show that the student is due to begin a certain activity in a few moments or go to a specialist in another room. The perspective is that the recovery process will take its own time and will not be accelerated, otherwise a regression to a meltdown may occur or the recovery process will be unnecessarily prolonged. It is most important to communicate that there is no urgency to resume the class activities and that the student is permitted to recover at her own pace.

Behavioral Responses to Probes Are the Key

The challenge is to know the status of the student in the recovery process. It is challenging for staff to know whether to push the student a little more by increasing the rate of tasks or directions. The dilemma is that if interactions are increased, the student may not be ready and may regress to another meltdown. If interactions are not increased, then the transition process may be lengthened. The key lies in presenting carefully chosen *probes* to the student. The idea is that an interaction involving a response from the student, such as a greeting, direction, or task, will provide clear information on what the student can manage at that particular stage of recovery. If the student responds positively to the interaction, then continue with further interactions. If the student pauses or does not respond, wait and give him a little more time and space. If the student reacts negatively to the probe, then withdraw and resume with the supportive measures used during the Meltdown Phase and give the student more time. In effect, the student's responses to these interactions will provide clear information on the status of the recovery. The application of such probes is described in more detail in the Intervention Steps section of this chapter.

Behavioral Indicators That a Meltdown Is Ending

Teachers and support staff know full well the serious impact that meltdowns can have on personnel, the involved student, other students, and the school in general. Consequently, it is very important to be ready to respond in a timely manner when the signs indicate that the meltdown is ending and the next phase, Re-Grouping, is beginning. Clearly, staff need precise indicators that this transition to recovery is beginning, otherwise the process may be lengthened unnecessarily or, worse still, the student may regress to a meltdown.

There are two clear signs that a student may be emerging from a melt-down. These signs can occur independently or, more commonly, in conjunction with each other: (a) reduction in behavioral intensity and (b) beginning responses to the environment

Reduction in Behavioral Intensity

As indicated by Figure 3.1: Six-Phase Model for the Cycle of Meltdowns of Students With ASD (see Chapter 3), the behavioral intensity is highest at the Meltdown Phase. For example, the scream-ing and yelling is significantly louder than in other phases; the thrashing on the floor, arm waving, and hand flapping are more intense; and tension in the student's body is much more pronounced than in any other phase.

The first indicator that a student is coming out of a meltdown is a reduction in behavioral *intensity*. For example, the student may be screaming quite loudly, then the screaming abates to crying, whining, or whimpering; the student may be shouting, then the shouting turns to mumbling or perseverative talk that is quieter; the student, instead of thrashing on the floor, may begin to sit still or lie more quietly on the floor. In general, there is an observable change in the student's behavior. The student is obviously still upset, but the intensity of the behavior has noticeably lessened.

Beginning Responses to the Environment

One of the defining characteristics of a meltdown is that the stu-dent is basically *oblivious* of anyone and anything in the environment. Consequently, when the student is coming out of a meltdown, one of the indicators is that she begins to respond to the environment. These responses may be quite subtle, such as the student beginning to look at the teacher or the supervising person, stare at an object in the room, or fiddle with some object. In some cases the student will manipulate or interact with something in the room, such as beginning to touch a chair, run her hand down the wall, or pick at the seams in her jacket. In general, the student is beginning to interact with the environment. However, it must be kept in mind that the student may still be quite disoriented and will appear confused and unfocused. This condition has important implications for how to interact with the student, which will be described in the Intervention Steps section of this chapter.

These two indicators, reduction in behavioral intensity and begin-ning responses to the environment, typically occur together. Once the behavioral intensity starts to diminish, the student begins to make small responses to the environment. It is at these moments that the teacher or supervising staff person initiates the intervention steps to facilitate the student's transition to recovery.

Intervention Steps

Once the student begins to show signs that the meltdown is abating (a reduction in behavioral intensity and responsiveness to the environment) the teacher or supervising person helps the student move toward recovery and resume the normal schedule. To accomplish this level of assistance, use *interaction probes* in a step-wise manner based on the student's responses.

Interaction probes are actions initiated by the teacher directed to the student, such as calling the student by name, asking a question, providing a simple choice (for example, "Do you want to sit here or over there?"), moving closer to the student, or inviting the student to participate in an activity that can be conducted in the room. If the student responds positively to such a probe, conclude that the student is attending to the environment and administer further interaction probes. However, if there is no response from the student or the student reacts negatively, withdraw, wait, provide supportive measures, and try again shortly with the probes.

Carefully manage the choice of interaction probes and specific intervention steps to ensure a smooth recovery, otherwise a meltdown may recur or the recovery period will be unduly prolonged. There are three important considerations involved in managing this part of the Re-Grouping Phase: (1) description of the transition model, (2) design of the interaction probes, and (3) implementation of progressive interaction probes.

Description of the Transition Model

The model for assisting the student in this phase is presented in Figure 8.1: Steps for Managing Transition From Meltdowns. The process begins with observing that the meltdown is ending (student's behavior shows a reduction in intensity, and responses to the environment begin to occur). The teacher then presents the first interaction probes, which need to be very simple and easy to complete, such as a greeting, moving closer to the student, presenting a straightforward request ("Michael come here please"), or handing something to the student and seeing if he takes it. Present these probes in a nonthreatening and relaxed manner. Watch the student closely to assess his response to the probes. If the student responds positively, such as looking over when the teacher calls his name or following the request, conclude that he is cooperating. Systematically introduce the progressive probes, leading to transition to the classroom and ultimately to participation in the current classroom activity (as depicted in the right-hand side of Figure 8.1). The specific stages for these progressive probes are described in the next section, Implementation of Progressive Interaction Probes.

However, withdraw slightly if the student shows resistance or reacts negatively to the initial probes, tell the student to wait a little longer, and return to using the supportive measures described for the Meltdown Phase. Do not communicate any degree of impatience, disappointment, or anxiety from thinking that the student should be cooperating at this point. Keep in mind that a meltdown is an intense

Figure 8.1   Steps for Managing Transition From Meltdowns

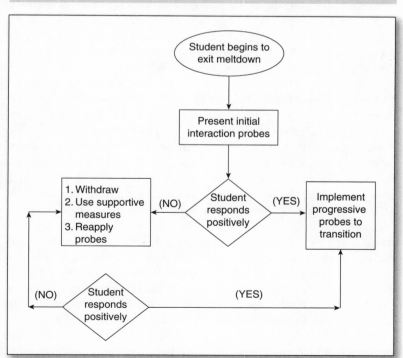

and often sustained difficult period for the student. Even though the student may appear to be calming down, he still may be very confused, and it will take more time for him to be sufficiently aware of what the teacher is presenting. Patiently use supportive measures to help the student calm down more. As he becomes calmer, resume presenting the interaction probes. Continue this cycle, as Figure 8.1 indicates, until the student responds positively to the initial interaction probes that set the stage for introducing the rest of the progressive probes. Do not be perturbed if this cycle continues a few times. The alternative is to take the student back to class, which is a much more difficult and demanding context, making it highly likely that another meltdown will recur.

Design of the Interaction Probes

It may seem a fairly straightforward procedure to administer interaction probes to a student to assist in the recovery process from a meltdown. It is not. It is particularly important to carefully design and select the interaction probes. The reason is that students with ASD have difficulty processing directions even when in a relatively calm state under normal conditions in the classroom. In this situation, however, they are emerging from a meltdown, when confusion prevails because of the associated turmoil. Follow these guidelines in designing and implementing interaction probes:

Sequence Probes From Simple to Complex. The initial probes need to be concrete, one-step interactions, such as a greeting or request to come here. The next stage involves expanding the probes to two or three steps. The complexity or number of steps systematically increases until the tasks and directions approximate those involved in the classroom instruction and activities. The level of difficulty should never exceed the skill level of the student. Students with limited skills at the lower end of the spectrum will need concrete, simple tasks accompanied by clear gestures. Students at the high end of the spectrum usually need clear, concrete tasks initially and then move to more complex tasks relatively quickly. Form 8.1: Sample Probes for the Re-Grouping Phase Across Spectrum Levels covers the range of abilities in the spectrum. Be sure to develop a short list of probes for your student beforehand so that after a meltdown you can administer the probes with reasonable fluency. To assist in developing specific probes for individual students, a blank version of Form 8.1 is presented in Appendix L.

Form 8.1   Sample Probes for the Re-Grouping Phase Across Spectrum Levels

Level in Spectrum	Initial Probes	Expanded Probes
Lower Level	"Michael, look here, please" and gestures by pointing to her face. "Thank you. Come here, please," pointing to nearby chair.	"Take this crayon, please, and put it on the desk." "Great." Hand student a worksheet from desk, point to drawing, and ask him to color circles.
Mid-Level	"Brandon, look here, please." "Thanks. What is your favorite TV show?"	"Tell me about this TV show you like." "Great, let's do some reading." Give student reading book and ask him to read.
Upper Level	"Emily, are you feeling better?" "Great, can we talk a little please?"	"So, it seems like you've had a rough day. Can you tell me, how are you feeling now?" "Can you write down what happened in the classroom?"

Build on Behavioral Momentum. The basic idea behind the design and implementation of the probes is the principle of behavioral momentum (described in Chapter 5). Essentially, when the student cooperates with one direction or request, then there is more chance of him cooperating with the next request. The probes are selected so that the student is likely to complete them successfully. This success, in turn, helps the student engage in subsequent probes. The key is to select probes that the student can complete successfully.

Track the Student's Responses Very Carefully. Pay close attention to how the student responds to the probes. If the response is correct, move forward with the probes. If the student does not respond correctly, withdraw, pause, and present a simpler probe. Once correct responding occurs, move forward in the sequence of probes. If the student reacts negatively by showing agitation, making noises, or pushing objects away, withdraw and adopt the supportive measures used earlier. Reintroduce the probes once the student has been given some space, becomes calmer, and shows signs of attending to the environment again.

Employ Communication Procedures Normally Used in the Classroom. Deliver the probes in the same mode of communication that is used in the classroom. If the student typically manages verbal directions and requests, then use the verbal mode. If the student needs visual cues, pictures, and gestures, then use visual supports in delivering the probes.

Develop Probes Beforehand and Review Frequently. Once it is known that a student has meltdowns, develop a list of interaction probes that could be used following a meltdown. The list helps to ensure that the probes are carefully selected, properly sequenced, and well within the response repertoire of the student. Moreover, by having familiar probes, the student is more likely to cooperate and to complete them successfully. The student becomes used to the routine. In addition, after the meltdown is over and the student has reentered the classroom, review the probes used, and modify as necessary.

Implementation of Progressive Interaction Probes

Now that the probes have been developed, the next step is to implement them in a systematic and progressive manner involving four broad stages. Each stage requires implementing more complex probes based on the successful completion of the previous probes, leading to participation in the regularly scheduled classroom activities. Clearly, these stages, and the number of them, will vary from student to student based on age level and the limitations related to each student's disability. The important point is that students typically recover from meltdowns in fairly observable stages. The teacher or adult needs to tune into these stages and work with them. Interaction probes are typically used by staff to determine where the student is in the recovery process, and the student's response to these probes will dictate what the teacher does next—either back up and give the student more time or proceed with the next steps toward recovery.

This section describes the respective steps for the Re-Grouping Phase (transition from a meltdown to the regular classroom schedule), which are followed by a checklist and action plan.

Step 1: Present Single-Step Interactions. These probes are simple interactions or requests (such as a greeting or a one-step request). They are spaced so that the student is not rushed and has sufficient time to process what is required of her.

Step 2: Expand the Interaction Tasks. There are three ways of expanding the interaction tasks:

   a. *Single-Step Probes.* Here, a series of single-step probes are presented, with faster pacing compared to the first stage. There is less time between the completion of a request and the presentation of the next request, that is, the pacing is increased.
   b. *Multiple-Step Interactions.* In this series the teacher presents requests or tasks that have more than one piece of information, for example, "(Student's name), would you come here, please, and sit down on this" or "(Student's name), please sit on this chair, and open the book to page 74." Naturally, the difficulty of the task requested must be within the response repertoire of the student. Some students, in the case of the previous example, would not be able to remember the page number, while others would not have the reading skills to find the page. The tasks must match the student's ability.
   c. *Longer-Duration Tasks.* These probes take more time to complete, which means that the student has to concentrate more and stay on task longer than in the previous probes. For example, the student could be asked to color in a figure, read a sentence or two from a book, write something down, or complete a simple puzzle.

Note: Students may need more or fewer probes based on their responses.

Step 3: Exit to a Preferred Activity in the Classroom. Now that the student has completed several interaction probes of increasing complexity, he can now reenter the classroom. Present this step in a particularly positive manner as something that has been accomplished. Your tone and whole demeanor is now a little more upbeat to signal the return to the classroom. Ensure that the entry activity is something very positive or enjoyable for the student—a preferred or special interest activity. There are two reasons for this choice. First, the student is still likely to be upset or a little confused to some extent following the meltdown. The preferred activity will help the student focus and become more settled. Second, the student may be somewhat fearful in leaving the relative security of the safe area with just the teacher and going to the usual high activity of the classroom with several people. Again, the preferred activity will help override this anxiety.

Step 4: Enter the Scheduled Classroom Activity. The final step in this process is to reenter the scheduled activity. It is presumed that by working through the previous steps, the student will be functioning at a sufficient level of cooperation and emotional stability to resume the classroom schedule and activities. Naturally, it is important to keep a close eye on the student to ensure she is getting sufficient attention and is performing acceptably.

Checklist and Action Plan

Form 8.2: Illustration of Checklist and Action Plan for Re-Grouping Phase addresses the steps in the process of the student's transition from a meltdown to the regular schedule. A blank version of the checklist and action plan is included in Appendix M.

Form 8.2   Illustration of Checklist and Action Plan for Re-Grouping Phase

---

Student Level: Mid-level on the spectrum, Brandon from Box 8.1

Step 1: Present single-step interactions

"Brandon, look here, please."

"Thanks. What is your favorite TV show?"

Step 2: Expand the interaction tasks

"Tell me about this TV show you like."

"Great, let's do some reading." Teacher gives him a reading book, and asks him to read.

Step 3: Exit to a preferred activity in the classroom

Following his successful reading of a couple of passages, teacher says in a positive tone, "Let's head back to class, and you can have a few minutes on the computer."

Brandon likes computer games. He enters classroom, goes to computer station, and begins playing one of his preferred games.

Step 4: Enter the scheduled classroom activity

After about 5 minutes, teacher acknowledges how well he is doing and then tells him that it is time to join the group for math.

Chapter Summary

The Re-Grouping Phase is a transition from the high-intensity behavior of a meltdown to the relative calm of recovery. This phase does not last very long, which means that the timing in applying strategies is crucial for a successful transition to the regular schedule to occur. The primary purpose of these strategies is to help the student regain composure, provide a focus on cooperation with the teacher, successfully complete a sequence of tasks, and transition smoothly to the regular classroom schedule.

The key assumption in this phase is that the student begins to become more responsive to the environment as she emerges from a meltdown. This shift enables the teacher to move from being a supportive presence in the Meltdown Phase to becoming more actively involved with the student by presenting interaction probes. The purpose of these probes is to systematically engage the student so that she can respond at first to a series of tasks that are initially simple and then to ones that are more complex, approximating the complexity of the classroom activities.

This chapter describes four stages leading to recovery. Each stage is designed to obtain increasing levels of cooperation so that when the student exits this phase, there is a reasonable chance that he will cooperate when he resumes normal activities in the classroom. It is most important to have specific probes in mind, or preferably on paper as in Form 8.1: Sample Probes for the Re-Grouping Phase Across Spectrum Levels, to assist the student in completing this phase and successfully resuming the classroom activities.

9

Starting-Over Phase

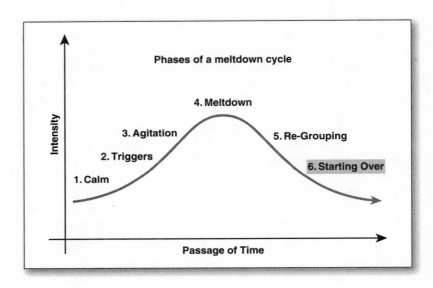

In this final phase, Starting Over, the student is back on the regular schedule. It is very important to understand that just because the student regained composure and was cooperating in the previous phase, Re-Grouping, there is no guarantee that the student will maintain cooperating and be free from problem behavior or even meltdowns. Granted, steps are systematically undertaken to help the student adjust to the regular setting following isolation in the safe area to minimize transition problems (Stages 3 and 4 of the intervention in the previous phase, Re-Grouping). However, the student, for the most part, regained composure and focus in another setting. That is, the student is coming from an isolated setting, in a one-to-one situation, and in an area with minimum noise. By contrast, the classroom usually involves more than one adult and several students, and typically involves more noise and movement than the safe area. Also, the original triggers that set off the meltdown more than likely are still present, such as the noise level or lighting, certain students or staff members, group work, or certain tasks. And there is always some chance that the other students may respond to the returning student in a way that is inflammatory (either deliberately or unwittingly). Consequently, additional steps and strategies need to be taken to assist the student in overcoming these potential problems related to resuming the normal class routines successfully.

In addition, students with autism spectrum disorder (ASD) who have meltdowns characteristically are quite deficient in self-regulation skills when it comes to managing emotions. Consequently, it will take time and consistent efforts to teach these students to effectively manage the events that typically trigger their meltdowns. Unfortunately, there does not appear to be a quick fix to provide these students with the skills to prevent meltdowns. Rather, staff are straddled with a slow process that involves systematically teaching students the self-regulation skills for managing their emotions when setbacks occur.

Moreover, meltdowns can be viewed as a quite destructive maladaptive response to certain triggers. The students are deficient in skills in crucial areas such as communication, cognition, socialization, and problem solving. Consequently, situations will inevitably arise in the classroom that cause problems, frustration, and confusion. Given that the students do not have the skills to prevent or manage these situations, they may exhibit strong emotional reactions leading to meltdowns.

The emphasis in this final phase, Starting Over, is to renew the efforts to teach these students the fundamental skills in the key areas for successful functioning in the classroom (self-regulation, communication, social competence, problem solving, and cognition). In this sense, this phase involves renewed efforts to teach these critical skills, with specific adjustments gleaned by carefully reviewing the previous meltdown.

The Starting-Over Phase has six main steps: (1) provide a strong emphasis on scheduled activities, (2) focus on scheduled transitions, (3) develop a debriefing plan, (4) shape sensory reactions, (5) heighten the emphasis on skill building, and (6) develop a comprehensive support plan. In this chapter, these steps are applied to two case studies. A checklist and action plan is presented at the end of the chapter.

Step 1: Provide a Strong Emphasis on Scheduled Activities

The immediate goal is to assist the student to reenter the classroom activity and maintain a high rate of on-task behavior in the current scheduled class activity (that is, as high as possible for the given student). Provide prompts, verbal reinforcement, contacts, and offers to assist as needed.

Sometimes a student may want to talk about the incident, such as what may have happened, who is at fault, and what happened to the other participants in the incident. In these cases it is best to assure the student that these issues, and others, will be fully addressed later on in the debriefing session.

It may also happen that the student will appear to be uncomfortable in class, look a little sheepish or embarrassed, show signs of agitation or confusion, and have difficulty participating in class. This situation could be confounded if the class is engaged in a challenging activity for the student, such as a group activity involving discussion or a project involving collaboration between students. In these cases, direct the student to an alternative interim activity and to join in the next scheduled activity that may be less challenging or threatening to the student.

Step 2: Focus on Scheduled Transitions

One of the well-known challenges facing students with ASD, especially those who are prone to meltdowns, is dealing with changes to their routines. It has been repeatedly mentioned throughout this book that disruptions of routines is one of the major triggers for problem behavior and meltdowns (see Chapters 3 and 5). The classroom schedule provides constant opportunities for these students to practice managing changes. The schedule indicates when the various subjects are being taught and when the multiple activities such as breaks, lunch, and recess are planned to occur. In a sense a school day can be seen as a series of activities requiring the student to make changes and adjust to transitions. In effect, the school day, with its many scheduled activities, is a prime learning opportunity for the student because of the many occasions to practice changing routines and, in some cases, disrupting the routines. The practice is even more important when the students are unable to finish a task during the set time and have to learn that these tasks will be finished at a later time. Essentially, they have to learn to manage disruptions.

Teachers of students with ASD who exhibit meltdowns are encouraged to pay particular attention to how these students manage these changes, or disruptions, brought about by the schedule. Some students will require additional assistance by receiving clear information ahead of time (advance prompts) that the present activity is about to finish. These prompts are even more important when the current activity will not be completed during the current scheduled time. Use the usual picture cues and symbols where necessary to help the student understand that the change is about to occur. Be ready to acknowledge and to provide appropriate reinforcement for students who cooperate with changing activities dictated by the schedule (especially in the case of students who often have difficulty with any changes to their routines).

Step 3: Develop a Debriefing Plan

One of the biggest issues facing students when they return to the classroom following a meltdown is that the same events or conditions that triggered the meltdown are likely to be present. This means that another meltdown could occur at some point. One powerful way to prevent this cycle is to include a *debriefing* activity that is designed to help the students understand the dynamics of the meltdown cycle and to prepare them to exhibit appropriate behavior in the future, especially in the presence of certain identified triggers. However, not all students will have the necessary cognitive skills to understand and benefit from this debriefing process. Essentially, the process may be appropriate for students who are at the high end of the spectrum. The student's responses during the debriefing process will provide information on whether or not the strategy is appropriate.

Debriefing is basically a feedback session, problem-solving meeting, or exit interview (Colvin, 2004). Generally, it is desirable to conduct the debriefing session after the student has been on track in the classroom for at least 20 minutes and preferably the same day as the occurrence of the meltdown. The session should take somewhere in the range of 5 to 10 minutes and be conducted in a quiet, separate area of the classroom.

The debriefing process is usually based on the following three questions:

1. What happened to make you upset?

2. What did you do when you became upset?

3. What could you do next time this happens?

For example, the student responses to these debriefing questions could be as follows:

1. What happened to make you upset?

"Another student would not let me finish on the computer."

2. What did you do when you became upset?

"I got mad and tried to tell him to wait. He wouldn't. Then I got madder and yelled at him. Then I had to leave the room."

3. What could you do next time this happens?

"Don't know. I could ask him to wait. I might start earlier or come back later. Maybe just quit and move on. Not sure."

Use a form in conducting the debriefing session based on these three questions. Depending on the student's ability level, either the student or the teacher fills out the form.

It is most important in conducting this debriefing process not to press too hard on accurate or complete responses as the student may become agitated again and have another meltdown. As long as some information is obtained, that is relatively close is all that is needed for this stage. Finally, be on the alert to catch any similar situations in the future that may have triggered escalation in the past so that the student is prompted or encouraged to use the alternative responses identified in the debriefing plan. Students often may not know what to do next time because they lack the coping or problem-solving skills. In these cases, it may take several trials or occurrences of meltdowns before the alternatives responses in the plan become effective.

Step 4: Shape Sensory Reactions

Sensory overload has been identified as another very common trigger for meltdowns. If this is the case for an individual student, then make adaptations in the classroom (for example, dimming the lights or reducing the number of lights to deal with bright lighting or creating quieter areas in the room if noise is a trigger).

However, in many situations in schools the sensory input cannot be altered, as is the case with noise in the cafeteria. In these cases use the strategy of *systematic shaping*. In general, the shaping strategy is designed to enable students to systematically adapt or acclimate from conditions with low sensory input to the full situation. For example, if a student has trouble with the noise level in the cafeteria, then the student's lunch schedule might be arranged so that he is in the cafeteria just before the first scheduled groups arrive. In this way the student experiences the space of the cafeteria and the gradual buildup of noise. The student would leave the cafeteria before the noise reaches its highest levels. Gradually, the student could come later to the cafeteria and stay longer depending on what he can handle.

Another student may strongly react to teacher interruptions and want to be left alone. But teachers need to check on students' work, their progress, whether or not they need help, and let the students know that time is up for certain activities. These are normal procedures in the classroom. However, what if a student reacts very strongly to any form of interruption and in some cases meltdowns have occurred? Shaping could be used to help the student respond appropriately to teacher presence or interactions. For example, at the beginning of an activity tell the student either orally or through picture cards that you will return in 3 minutes, signaling 3 minutes on the clock or picture. In 3 minutes return and watch the student closely to assess her level of reaction. Determine how long to stay, and at what level to interact with the student or not, based on the student's previous reaction. This procedure will continue until the student is more comfortable with you approaching her during an activity.

Step 5: Heighten the Emphasis on Skill Building

Frustrations and problems arising from skill deficits in critical classroom areas can also trigger behavioral concerns and meltdowns, specifically the skill areas of cognition, language or communication, and social competence (as described more fully in Chapters 1 and 3). The key to addressing this class of triggers involves *quality instruction* using *research-based curricula* for these essential skill areas. Clearly, if students with ASD can be taught to identify and manage their feelings (emotion regulation skills), understand what is required of them (cognitive skills), communicate what they need (language skills), and get along with their peers (social competence), they will not only be successful in school with their learning but also be far less likely to have significant behavioral issues leading to meltdowns.

Teachers are encouraged to always be on the lookout for effective instructional delivery systems, sound curricula, and professional development opportunities for material to enhance the skills of these vulnerable students. Mastery of these core skills is crucial to success in school and behavior control.

Step 6: Develop a Behavior Support Plan

So far in the Starting-Over Phase of the cycle of meltdown behavior, emphasis has been placed on the initial reentry to the classroom to ensure a smooth transition from the safe area following a meltdown to the regular schedule in the classroom. If several meltdowns have occurred for a student, which unfortunately is reasonably common, then a comprehensive behavior support plan needs to be developed, otherwise the cycle of meltdowns will continue. There are four parts to this section: (1) clarification of approach, (2) behavioral assessment, (3) identification of specific strategies, and (4) application to case studies.

Clarification of Approach

It is standard practice in developing behavior support plans for high-needs students to use variations of functional behavior assessments (FBAs). You may wonder why this process is not highlighted in this section. There are several reasons for this decision. First, the bulk of published research in using FBAs to develop behavior support plans has focused on students with intellectual disabilities, predominantly younger children (Gadaire, Kelley, & DeRosa, 2010). Second, behaviors of concern for children with ASD, as with childhood psychoses and schizophrenia, have been depicted as *internalizing behavior problems* directed inward (as distinct from externally directed behavior such as acting out, tantrums, and aggression; Walker, Ramsey, & Gresham, 2003). Again, published research on students with internalizing and externalizing problems has centered almost exclusively on externalizing problems (Kern, Hilt, & Gresham, 2004). Third, the limited published research on using FBAs for students with ASD has been restricted to classification and assessment rather than intervention (Gresham & Kern, 2004). Finally, in an extensive review of studies that focused on students with ASD, it was reported that there is no difference in outcomes in using strategies with or without FBAs (Machalicek, O'Reilly, Beretvas, Sigafoos, & Lancioni, 2007).

It is clear that much more research needs to be done to determine the applicability and utility of using FBAs in developing behavior support plans for students with ASD. For these reasons, our core approach in developing a behavior support plan for students with ASD is to focus on systematically noting the behaviors of the students as they progress through the six phases of the meltdown cycle and apply specific strategies at the onset of these behaviors. In effect, the behavior support plan incorporates interventions for *each of the six phases* in the meltdown cycle.

Behavioral Assessment

Chapter 3 described the meltdown cycle in terms of six phases (Calm, Triggers, Agitation, Meltdown, Re-Grouping, and Starting Over). Specific behaviors were identified for each phase of this model, and behavioral descriptions were culled from a large sample of students who exhibit this behavioral pattern. The primary purpose of classifying behavior in this way is to enable practitioners to observe and respond to the behavioral processes involved in escalating situations for students with ASD that lead to and follow meltdowns. The descriptions tell the teachers which student behavior to expect at each stage in the meltdown cycle, which in turn dictates the strategies to use for interventions. The first step in developing a behavior support plan is to identify the key behaviors an individual student exhibits for each of the six phases, the *assessment* component.

Note: Appendix A: Summary and Checklist for Behaviors of Each Phase in the Meltdown Cycle (which is the same as Form 3.1) provides an overview of the characteristic behaviors of each phase in the conceptual model of the meltdown cycle for students with ASD. This list serves as a basis for identifying the specific behaviors for an individual student.

Identification of Specific Strategies

Once the behaviors have been determined for each of the six phases in the meltdown cycle, the next step is to identify specific *strategies* to be used in each of these phases. These strategies are implemented at the onset of behaviors observed from the first step, assessment. The basic intent of the strategies is to arrest the behavior at that point in the cycle, thereby preventing further escalation and, at the same time, setting the stage for students to engage in appropriate alternative behavior. The overall emphasis is on identifying the early behaviors in the cycle, redirecting the students toward appropriate behavior, and subsequently preempting the occurrence of a meltdown. In first three phases (Calm, Triggers, and Agitation), the emphasis is on effective teaching and proactive management practices. In the remaining phases (Meltdown, Re-Grouping, and Starting Over) the emphasis is in safety, crisis management, and follow-up.

Appendix B: Behavior Support Plan (which is the same as Form 3.2) is designed for developing a comprehensive behavior support plan for students who exhibit repeated meltdowns. The left-hand column of the form, labeled Assessment, is used to list the characteristic behaviors the student exhibits at each phase of the meltdown cycle. The right-hand column of the form, labeled Strategies, identifies the specific interventions selected to be used for each phase. The form is completed for the following two case studies.

Application to Case Studies

We return now to the behavior support plan for two students introduced in Chapter 3, Ricky and Elena. At that point the assessment part of their behavior support plans was completed. The other component, strategies corresponding to each phase in the meltdown cycle, is now added to complete the plans. Ideally, each plan would be completed at a meeting involving the parents and all personnel who work with the student. A recapitulation of each student's behavioral history is provided in Boxes 9.1. and 9.2, followed by a completed behavior support plan for each student in Boxes 9.3 and 9.4.

Note: The home-based component of this behavior support plan will be described in Chapter 10 (Box 10.5: Home-Based Behavior Support Plan for Ricky).

| Box 9.1 | Case Study 1: Recap of Ricky's Behavioral History |

Ricky is a 5-year-old boy with autism. He never initiates conversations and rarely makes eye contact with other individuals. He has difficulty communicating with his peers and usually does not respond when people speak to him. On a regular basis, Ricky becomes upset and has serious meltdowns with screaming, throwing things around, rushing around the room, and flailing his arms. His parents report that his behavior at school and at home has worsened in that he is having more meltdowns since they moved to a different area of town and a new school. Presently, he is placed in a special education class at the local elementary school. His teacher reports that she has been unable to find effective teaching strategies to work with Ricky. She says that he is very disruptive in class when he has his meltdowns and that she has to remove the rest of the class to an adjacent room so that teaching can continue and he can calm down. At this stage she has been unable to identify the triggers, and when he does escalate, it goes very fast.

| Box 9.2 | Case Study 2: Recap of Elena's Behavioral History |

Elena is a 15-year-old girl with Asperger syndrome. She does best when teachers and staff respond to her interests. She likes to talk about her hobbies, such as her card collection of pop singers, and talks with more animation when staff show interest by responding to her comments. She can stay focused for lengthy periods, especially with tasks that are routine and have definite closure, such as completing a page of writing or math. She enjoys independent activities such as computer games and watching TV or video programs and games.

Elena has little interest in socializing with children her own age. She tends to talk about her area of interest (TV stars, especially female singers) and does not pay any attention to what the other person might be talking about. Her speech is overly formal and pedantic, and she loves to relay factual information about her favorite singers, the songs they sing, and when you can watch them on TV. She does very well when she does what she wants to do, but if her routines are interrupted or staff try to follow through with getting her to participate in activities she does not like, she becomes very physical, banging things around and screaming, and basically has a meltdown.

| Box 9.3 | Behavior Support Plan for Ricky |

Student Name: Ricky Wiley   Date: 4/3/11
Teacher: Mary-Sharon Weatherspoon   Grade: 1
Staff Present: Josephine Wardley, Tom Scruggs,
Ellen Hawthorne, and Mary-Sharon Weatherspoon

Assessment	Strategies
Calm	**Calm**
Works well when left alone	*Rearrange seating to reduce*
Stays working once started	*distractions*

(Continued)

(Continued)

Assessment	Strategies
Accepts assistance, follows directions, and concentrates for long periods Can transition when previous task is completed Receives praise related to tasks	Expand visual cue use Teach use of visual cues in requesting assistance
Triggers	**Triggers**
The movement when other students were crowding around the front of the class The noise level from the front of the class The approach of the teacher assistant The transition from what Ricky was engaged in to reading	Evaluate use of earphones Train staff on less intrusive way to approach Provide advance prompts (picture cues) for transitions
Agitation	**Agitation**
Ricky skips Phase III: Agitation and goes straight to Phase IV: Meltdown.	Presently not applicable
Meltdown	**Meltdown**
Sustained screaming Running to the corner of the room Falling on the floor Thrashing his legs Flailing his arms	Guide to designated safe area Conduct room clear if needed Provide space and monitor safety Use supportive measures Follow emergency protocol as necessary
Re-Grouping	**Re-Grouping**
Screaming began to subside Sat on floor with hands over ears Responded to prompt to build with Legos Built house of Legos	Identify reduction in intensity and increasing awareness Continue supportive measures Begin interaction probes

Assessment	Strategies
Starting Over	**Starting Over**
Worked with the Legos	*Transition to preferred activity*
Followed direction to join group	*Guide to scheduled activity*
Sat in group but did not participate	*Maintain supportive measures*
	Resume skill instruction
	Increase emphasis on functional communication skills

Box 9.4   Behavior Support Plan for Elena

Student Name: Elena Warner   Date: 6/18/11

Teacher: Josh Parkinson   Grade: 10

Staff Present: Angela Timms, Joe Barkley, Josh Parkinson, Marietta Coley, and Francis McMahon

Assessment	Strategies
Calm	**Calm**
Works best when teachers show interest in her work	*Increase teacher contact when on task*
Talks about hobbies and interests	*Provide clearer visual information on task closure*
Stays on task with set routines with definite closure	*Increase independent work*
Works well when left alone	
Stays focused with computer games	
Triggers	**Triggers**
Had to stop sorting her cards when she was not finished; routine was interrupted	*Provide advance prompts for transitions*
The teacher's persistence with finishing up	*Increase incentives for successful transitions*
	Negotiate some flexibility with tasks not finished

(Continued)

(Continued)

Assessment	Strategies
The teacher touching and moving one of her cards	Rehearse options for exiting high-interest activities
Agitation	**Agitation**
Putting head down	Provide space
Moving cards more quickly	Present choices
Mumbling	Remain calm and unhurried
	Provide encouragement
Meltdown	**Meltdown**
Grabbing cards	Guide to safe area
Kicking furniture	Conduct room clear if needed
Shouting and screaming	Provide space and monitor safety
Pounding on walls	Use supportive measures
Ripping materials	Follow emergency procedures only if needed
Sustained screaming	
Re-Grouping	**Re-Grouping**
Sat down still upset	Identify reduction in intensity and increasing awareness
Began to sort cards	
Folded arms, stared at floor	Continue supportive measures
Completed form	Begin interaction probes
Cooperated with directions to join class	Be ready for quick recovery
Starting Over	**Starting Over**
Resumed class activity	Transition to preferred activity
Cooperated with debriefing	Resume scheduled activity
Somewhat subdued and mumbled a lot	Debrief
	Increase emphasis on coping and problem-solving skills
	Use shaping to increase tolerance for interruptions

Checklist and Action Plan

At this juncture the teacher and staff are typically quite relieved that the student has recovered from the meltdown and is back on track with the regular schedule. However, it is most important to carefully monitor and review actions taken by staff in following procedures as the student reenters the classroom. The following checklist, Form 9.1: Illustration for Checklist and Action Plan for Starting Over, is designed to help teachers assess the steps they took following a student's meltdown and reentry in the classroom schedule. A blank version is included in Appendix N: Checklist and Action Form for Starting Over.

Form 9.1   Illustration for Checklist and Action Plan for Starting Over

Student Level: High end of spectrum, verbal, average intellectual functioning, elementary

Step 1: Provide a Strong Emphasis on Scheduled Activities

Provide strong positive reinforcement for participating in reading group. Give the student as many turns as possible, and ensure the student is dealing with material with which he will be successful.

Monitor the student very carefully for any signs of agitation or confusion. Provide immediate assistance and, if necessary, change the activity and resume later.

Step 2: Focus on Scheduled Transitions

Be especially aware of difficulties the student may have with initial transitions. Monitor closely, and provide assistance or contact as necessary. Maintain high levels of reinforcement for cooperation.

Step 3: Develop a Debriefing Plan

Develop a standard form around "What did you do? Why did you do it? What else could you do?"

Schedule debriefing time.

Discuss the incident, and have the student complete a form with assistance as needed.

Step 4: Shape Sensory Reactions

This particular student was triggered by an announcement over the PA when he was engaged in silent reading.

Focus practice on reading with short teacher interruptions, such as asking a question or telling him what will happen during PE.

Just before announcement time over the PA, remind the student of the need to stop what he is doing and listen to the announcement.

(Continued)

(Continued)

Step 5: Heighten the Emphasis on Skill Building

In this example the emphasis is on problem solving. Plan options for the student to follow and initiate when something disturbs him (go to quiet area, use head phones, etc.)

Step 6: Develop a Behavior Support Plan

If repeated meltdowns occur, develop a full support plan for the student, identifying behaviors and interventions for each of the six phases in the cycle of meltdowns. (See Appendix B: Behavior Support Plan.)

Chapter Summary

The overall objective for the strategies in the Starting-Over phase is to continue the transition from the Re-Grouping phase to full participation in the current classroom activities and to make some changes to help the students respond appropriately to future events. The debriefing process is designed for students who exhibit meltdowns and who are at the higher end of the spectrum. The debriefing strategy helps the students pinpoint the critical events that may have contributed to the meltdown incident and helps the teacher establish acceptable replacement behaviors for similar situations in the future. If sensory-overload triggers are involved, then make adjustments in the classroom to attenuate the sensory effects, where practical. In other cases, the strategy of systematic shaping helps the students build more tolerance to troubling sensory conditions. An overriding and long-term intervention for students with ASD who exhibit meltdowns is to provide them with ongoing effective instruction in critical areas for success in school—specifically skill development in the areas of emotions, cognition, communication, and social competence.

Students who display meltdown behavior on a regular basis need a comprehensive behavior support plan, which can be developed based on the six phases of the meltdown cycle. The first step in the plan, the assessment component, is to identify the characteristic behaviors the student displays for each of the six phases. The second step, the strategies component, involves using specific strategies designed for each phase. The basic approach is that once the characteristic behaviors are exhibited by the student, teachers and staff implement corresponding strategies for each phase. A simple two-part form is used to identify each of these steps for the phases in the meltdown cycle.

10

The Parent Component

It is essential for teachers of students with autism spectrum disorder (ASD) who have meltdowns to include the parents in all phases of the development and implementation of the behavior support plan. Both parents and teachers have complementary information to offer. Parents can provide teachers with important information about their child's behaviors at home and what they have found helpful, while teachers can provide parents with information about what works best at school. The ideal situation is one in which educators and parents work in close collaboration to systematically develop a comprehensive behavior support plan. In this way students receive a coordinated and consistent plan for addressing meltdown behavior in all key settings—at school, in the home, and in the community.

However, such an in-depth, collaborative, and give-and-take partnership will not occur by chance. Moreover, the traditional school structures for teachers and parents to work together, such as parent conferences and reports, will not be adequate. The purpose of this chapter is to provide teachers and support personnel with information on the *parent component* in the development and implementation of a comprehensive behavior support plan. The topics addressed are (1) benefits of parent-teacher collaboration, (2) challenges in building parent-teacher partnerships, and (3) steps for building parent-teacher partnerships.

Benefits of Parent-Teacher Collaboration

The number-one factor contributing to stress in parents of children with ASD is the presence of challenging behaviors such as meltdowns, temper tantrums, aggression, and self-abuse (Osborne & Reed, 2009; Tehee, Honan, & Hevey, 2009). Raising a child with any chronic illness or disability is very difficult and demanding. However, the distinct challenges posed by children with ASD who have meltdowns place this group of parents at an especially high risk for psychological challenges (Schieve, Blumberg, Rice, Visser, & Boyle, 2007).

Teachers can be of immeasurable help to these parents by providing them with support, information, and training on how to help manage their child's disruptive and troublesome behaviors at home and in the community. Parents are often focused on what their child is doing at the present moment and generally do not have the opportunity, and sometimes the background knowledge, to step back and examine the detailed patterns associated with these behaviors. Teachers can be particularly helpful to parents in explaining how their child's behavior can be described in terms of a cycle with six fairly discrete phases. By using illustrations teachers can help parents track what is going on in a meltdown and especially what can be done at each phase in the cycle. Just the very act of understanding what is happening in the cycle can provide both relief and direction to parents.

Similarly, parents can be a highly valuable resource to teachers who are trying to develop an effective intervention for the student at school (Moyes, 2002). Parents have the opportunity to see how the child behaves and responds under conditions at home, which are very different from those at school. Consequently, the parents' observations and strategies can be of significant importance for teachers in the development of a behavior support plan for the student. Moreover, parents have an intimate knowledge of their child and obviously are the key players in their child's life. They have lived with their child for 24 hours a day, 7 days a week since he or she was born. They are often more tuned into the subtle changes that occur and know what may bother or please their child. Consequently, when the teacher is identifying observable factors for each of the six phases in the cycle of meltdown behavior, parents can share what they see and experience at home for each phase. They know what their child is likely to engage in during the Calm Phase, what triggers the disruptive behaviors, what is effective at times in defusing the situation. Parents are in a strong position to provide pertinent information on each phase in the meltdown cycle.

Challenges in Building Parent-Teacher Partnerships

While there is a compelling logic for parents and teachers to work together in a constructive partnership, it is not that easy to accomplish. A major reason is that a number of factors inhibit such relationships. These factors, if present, need to be identified and resolved in order for fruitful collaboration to occur. Moreover, if teachers are aware of these inhibiting factors, then they can take measures to prevent roadblocks or problems from occurring.

It is also very important for teachers and educators to understand that these inhibiting factors can arise unwittingly. That is, teachers may be totally unaware that what they are saying or doing may cause a rift with the parents or confirm a rift that is already there. Teachers may be operating in the *business as usual mode,* while the parents may have different perceptions. For example, the parents may feel threatened, ignored, or put down by what is being said or done. There is no suggestion in this section that teachers are at fault. Rather, the message is that the stress from having a having a child with ASD who exhibits meltdowns can distort parents' perceptions. Consequently, teachers may need to be on the alert and take extra steps to ensure that their actions are not misinterpreted.

Commonly identified inhibiting factors include (a) negative history with schools, (b) use of technical language, (c) feeling blame, (d) condescending attitude, (e) inflexibility or insensitivity in scheduling meetings, (f) unreasonable expectations, (g) use of medication, and (h) dealing with outbursts and mending bridges.

Negative History With Schools

In some cases, parents have had bad experiences in working with schools (Smith Myles & Southwick, 2005). For example, parents may feel they have been given the runaround or treated disrespectfully on earlier occasions when trying to get services for their child or another child. In addition, some parents may have had negative experiences themselves when they were in school. Consequently, when they become involved with the teacher or new situation, they already have the disposition that the school is not really out to help them or their child. They believe that they have to fight for everything they get. In effect, the school has become an adversary rather than a friend.

Use of Technical Language

It is very easy for a teacher to fall into the trap of using technical language that is commonly used in educational circles but not in homes (Walker, Ramsey, & Gresham, 2003). Consequently, when teachers talk to parents, what they say is often not understood. Also, parents may be disinclined to seek clarification because they feel they will come across as uneducated or "stupid." In addition, when teachers ask parents if they understand what is said, the parents may nod in agreement rather than admit they do not understand. Unfortunately, when the exchange is completed, the teacher thinks she is understood, and the parents leave knowing they did not understand.

Feeling Blame

One of the most difficult perceptions to deal with in trying to establish solid partnerships is when parents sense they are to blame for their child's behavior. They feel they are not raising their child correctly. Or some parents believe that the teachers and administrators think it is the parents' fault that the child has these meltdowns that disrupt the classroom and school. Occasionally, teachers are shocked to learn that the parents sense they are blamed for their child's behavior when the teachers feel they try so hard not to communicate blame. Moreover, some parents may not feel blame so much as a strong sense of embarrassment and powerlessness over the situation.

Condescending Attitude

Another difficult perception commonly reported is that parents feel they are talked down to and that there is an undertone of condescension when educators relate to them. Parents are well aware that the teachers and educators have their degrees, while in some cases the parents did not complete high school. The teachers and educators may come across as experts, and their role is to educate the parents on the complexities of ASD. Again, teachers may be unaware of these perceptions and unaware that their behavior with the parents may exacerbate the problem.

Parents sometimes report that they are not listened to in meetings or that their opinion is not valued. They begin to say something and are interrupted, or when they finish a comment no one at the meeting responds to what they have said and simply move onto something else. They sense their input is not important.

Inflexibility or Insensitivity in Scheduling Meetings

A key to establishing a fruitful partnership between teachers and parents is to conduct regular meetings. However, one barrier, which again could be a perception issue, is that teachers may not pay sufficient attention to the logistics involved for parents in getting to meetings. Insufficient flexibility may be shown in setting up the meetings. Parents often have to deal with child care, transportation, work schedules, family sickness, meal preparation, and other family constraints that make it difficult to attend meetings, especially after school. Clearly, if it is a hardship for the parents to attend meetings, then it will be that much more difficult to establish a productive partnership between the parents and their child's teachers.

Unreasonable Expectations

An aware teacher will know what can reasonably be expected from parents in working together. However, in some cases parents are asked to do more than they can competently handle. Thus, when the expectations are not met, the parents feel the burden of failure and the teachers feel that the parents are not cooperating.

As with any group of parents, there is a wide range in background, educational levels, financial needs, family size, support, cultural norms, and mental and intellectual capacities in parents of children with ASD. Consequently, there is no place for a one-size-fits-all approach in working with parents. Just as the child has individual needs and unique abilities, so do the parents. These differences, if not accommodated, will inhibit the effectiveness of the parent-teacher partnership.

Use of Medication

A common source of aggravation for parents and school personnel is the management of the child's medication. Parents have complained that teachers exert pressure on them to seek medication for their child. Teachers are often concerned that the child is overmedicated or medicated irregularly. Clearly, teachers and parents need to be on the same page regarding the use of medication, and they need to communicate regularly concerning changes in dosage levels and corresponding changes in the child's behavior.

Dealing With Outbursts and Mending Bridges

It does not take much reflection to appreciate that a child with ASD who has meltdowns can impose severe stress on families and school personnel (Neff, 2011; Woodcock & Page, 2010). As a result, there may be some heated or tense exchanges at a meeting. While these situations are certainly undesirable, spur-of-the-moment exchanges can occur that may lead to a rift in the parent-teacher relationship. It is important, especially for the child's sake, that efforts are undertaken to work through these kinds of problems if they arise.

Steps for Building Parent-Teacher Partnerships

It is clear that the when teachers and parents collaborate effectively, students have much more chance of being successful at school and at home (B. Ingersoll & Dvortcsak, 2010; Walker et al., 2003). Parent-teacher partnerships ensure more consistency in procedures for establishing desirable behavior and in addressing problem behavior for students with ASD. However, given the potential roadblocks and inhibiting factors identified in the previous section of this chapter, teachers and parents need to take definite steps for this kind of quality partnership to be developed.

We recommend that teachers use the following 10 steps to establish effective teacher-parent partnerships: (1) build trust, (2) involve parents in the plan, (3) overcome logistical constraints for parents and team members, (4) establish ongoing communication, (5) monitor teacher-parent interactions, (6) support the parents in implementing the home program, (7) track results, (8) celebrate progress, (9) provide professional support to parents, and (10) develop home-based component of behavior support plan.

Step 1: Build Trust

The first step in developing a positive and cooperative relationship with parents is to build trust. Other words often used to capture this underlying basis for establishing a strong partnership are *rapport*, *positive regard*, and *mutual respect*. Strive to communicate three key elements of establishing trust with parents:

1. *Have the best interests of the student at heart.* While this should be a given, explicitly state this goal and state it repeatedly. Parents soon pick up whether or not a teacher is keenly interested in their child succeeding at school. The converse is also true.

Communicate a genuine interest in the student by knowing his strengths and successes, and where he needs special help.

2. *Sincerely speak to the importance of working closely together.* The message is that both parents and teachers need each other and must work in tandem for the child to succeed at school and at home. Respond positively to the parents, actively listen to them, use the information provided by them, encourage suggestions, and act on these suggestions to set the stage for a solid partnership. Finally, give parents adequate time to express themselves, and avoid rushing them. Many parents, unlike teachers, may not have had much experience in speaking in a group situation, as some may not have had much opportunity, unlike teachers, or the need to speak in a group of professionals.

3. *Demonstrate trustworthiness.* Some parents need to be convinced that the teachers are trustworthy. Understand that trustworthiness is established by action and not just words alone. Seize opportunities, especially early on, to follow through with tasks and expectations. When parents see that the teacher means business by following through, they are more likely to trust them. This is even more important when parents have had negative experiences in the past or are skeptical of assistance that schools provide.

Step 2: Involve Parents in the Plan

Recognize that parents need to actually *experience* that they are contributing partners in working with teachers. Actively involve the parents in the planning and development of the behavior support plan as much as possible. Ideally, sit down with the parents and use Appendix A: Summary and Checklist for Behaviors of Each Phase in the Meltdown Cycle to explain the cycle some time before the scheduled planning meeting. Briefly illustrate each phase, and solicit examples from the parents to ensure that the meltdown cycle is understood. Explain the form used to develop a plan (Appendix B: Behavior Support Plan), and describe the two main sections for each phase, *assessment* and *strategies.* At this juncture invite input from the parents, and pencil in their suggestions. Leave the form with the parents so that each phase can be completed in their own time at home. The parents would then bring the completed form to the scheduled meeting. The purpose of the meeting would then be to develop a behavior support plan with input from the parents.

At all costs, avoid talking *at* the parents in the planning meeting. Parents need to be made to feel that they are an essential part of the team. View the parents as a source of important knowledge, and treat them as a valuable resource in the process. In this way the parents then will be more willing to share information that will be valuable in the development of the behavior support plan (Sicile-Kira, 2004).

Finally, even though the meeting is called to address meltdown behavior, begin the meeting with a discussion on the child's strengths. By starting with the Calm Phase, the discussion centers on the student's strengths, which helps to foster positive interactions with the parents and the entire team. Even though the parents are well aware their child has significant behavior problems, they also know the child has many strengths and are encouraged when they see the teacher acknowledging these strengths.

Step 3: Overcome Logistical Constraints for Parents and Team Members

Be aware of logistical factors facing the parents, and schedule meetings at a time and location convenient for them. Use flexibility in arranging the meeting to accommodate the needs of the parents and team members. While a meeting after school may be convenient for the teaching staff, it can be very difficult for the parents, who may be working, waiting for their other children to come home, or rearranging afterschool care and transportation. Consider these factors carefully in planning the meeting, and be willing to meet at other times of the day that are more favorable for the parents. By being aware of these constraints and making the necessary accommodations, teachers give parents a clear message that their presence at the meeting is highly valued (the converse is also true).

Step 4: Establish Ongoing Communication

By establishing an ongoing communication system with regular and timely contact, teachers are in a stronger position to catch problems early, provide timely support to parents as needed, gauge the effectiveness of the behavior support plan in case minor adjustments need to be made, and provide overall encouragement to the team. There are many ways to achieve this level of communication, such as letters, notes, phone calls, text messages, e-mail messages, handwritten messages on school notices (newsletters or school bulletins), or a quick visit at the start or end of the school day. In some cases parents may drop in for a short visit during the school day. The key is to use communication procedures that ensure regular and timely contact.

Step 5: Monitor Teacher-Parent Interactions

Constantly monitor the quality of interactions with the parents. It is possible to unwittingly turn off parents by coming across as "the expert," rushing the parents, interrupting their comments, using condescending tones or language, or simply talking too much. One way of monitoring these interactions is to pose a question to another team member and follow up after the meeting on the team member's perceptions. Or, more directly, ask the parents at the end of the meeting how they felt they were treated, if they felt comfortable expressing their opinions, and whether or not they felt like a valued member of the team. Just by asking the question, you give parents information that you are trying to foster positive interactions.

Step 6: Support the Parents in Implementing the Home Program

The ideal behavior support plan for managing and preventing meltdown behavior has a component to be implemented at school and another component to be implemented in the home and community (see Step 10). Inform parents on how the plan is working at school, and also provide support for the home-based component of the plan. Implementing the plan at home may require changes in the way parents work with or manage their child. Be prepared to make several reminders and offer words of encouragement to assist parents in making these changes at home. In addition, especially early on, be ready to field questions the parents may have and be sensitive to the fact that the home environment is substantially different from school and that certain accommodations may need to be made. It is important that the parents sense that the teacher is a support person rather than someone who is overprescriptive on how to be a parent. Be ready to assist the parents in making modifications to the plan, especially if there are too many difficulties with implementing the procedures. Similarly, modifications may need to be made if there is an increase in frequency or intensity with the meltdowns at home or in the community. For example, TVs and video games can be turned down; quiet areas can be identified; rooms can be rearranged to minimize distractions; and visual schedules, communication boards, and environmental labels can all be adjusted or introduced. Parents are most likely well aware of sensory issues with their child, and both the teacher and parents can brainstorm ideas on adjustments that can be made at home. It may also be helpful to talk to school specialists such as speech therapists, social workers, counselors, occupational therapists, and ASD consultants for ideas that parents can use at home. There always should be a strong emphasis on strategies that strengthen what the parent does during the Calm Phase. The same brainstorming process can be applied to each phase of the meltdown cycle of the behavior support plan.

Finally, and most important, stay in close contact with parents in the early stages of the intervention. It is usually here that problems arise and adjustments need to be made in a timely manner.

Step 7: Track Results

One very important topic to be addressed at the meeting is how to track results. Teachers and parents need to know if progress is being made with the behavior support plan. Is the plan working or not? The tracking system also enables teachers and parents to make decisions about whether to maintain the plan, to modify it, or in some cases to start over and develop a new plan. Typically there are two aspects of a behavior support plan that are tracked: (a) fidelity of implementation and (b) changes in the student's behavior.

Fidelity of implementation simply answers the question: Is the behavior support plan being implemented as intended or as agreed upon? Clearly, it is pointless to talk about the student's behavior if the plan is not being followed. Place strong emphasis on the importance of following the details of the plan with the parents and all team members

Within the behavior support plan, there are six phases depicting the meltdown cycle. Usually, one or two specific strategies are identified for use in each phase in both the school plan and the home plan (see illustration in Step 10). The simplest way of measuring fidelity of implementation is to ask the question: Is the designated strategy of the plan being implemented? The responses can be *yes, no,* or *sometimes.* Discuss the particular responses with the parents and team members. If the responses are *yes,* acknowledge the parents' effort and encourage them to continue. If the responses are *no* or *sometimes,* examine with the parents possible reasons or roadblocks that may be unforeseen and make adjustments as necessary. Or oftentimes the parents may forget to use the strategies because the plan is new to them. In this case, simply encourage the parents to do their best to remember and follow the plan. Also understand the importance of the parents needing to change their behavior first before changes in the student's behavior can occur.

Follow up with the parents shortly after the planning meeting to assess fidelity of implementation by means of the communication system that has been established. Conduct a more formal review of fidelity of implementation at the first follow-up meeting.

Changes in student behavior addresses whether the behavior support plan is working or not. During the planning meeting the team members agree on what is measured to let everyone know if the plan is effective or making a difference. The easiest and most obvious measures relate to aspects of the meltdowns. The simplest approach is to ask the parents to track three measures of meltdowns:

1. *Frequency*—how often the meltdowns occur (daily or weekly)

2. *Duration*—how long the meltdowns last (usually in minutes)

3. *Intensity*—how invasive or severe the meltdown is, which is sometimes hard to gauge. A useful approach is for parents to use a scale of 1 to 10, where 10 is the worst-case scenario involving loud screaming, banging things, attempts to injure, and very high states of agitation, and 1 is the lowest level, involving mumbling, perseveration with movement or speech, self-stimulation, and withdrawal.

These data or measures provide very important information on whether or not the plan is working and provide a basis for *decisions* to be made regarding the plan. Give the plan at least 3 or 4 weeks to see whether or not it is effective. It generally takes 2 weeks or so for parents and staff to implement the plan consistently and then 2 weeks or more to determine if it works. At this juncture, depending on the data, make decisions on whether to maintain, modify, or develop a new plan.

Moderate the parents' expectations if necessary. Parents, understandably, may want a *quick fix* to bring their child's behavior under control as soon as possible so they can enjoy home life more and not have to deal with these highly intrusive meltdowns. Set realistic expectations of what can be accomplished and how long it may take. Parent support groups can also be very helpful in this regard (see Step 9).

Finally, explain to parents that progress is determined by considering all three measures—frequency, duration, and intensity—sometimes separately and sometimes together. For example, the frequency of the meltdowns may remain the same or even increase, but the duration or intensity may substantially decrease, which would be seen as progress.

Step 8: Celebrate Progress

Much has been said in this chapter about the need for teachers and parents to work together, develop a strong partnership based on mutual trust, and contribute to the behavior support plan. One particularly important way for teachers to enhance the parent-teacher partnership is to celebrate progress. When the student makes changes in her behavior, such as a reduction in the intensity, duration, or frequency of the meltdowns, organize a small event to acknowledge the progress. The event can simply be a gathering with cake and juice before school or anytime that works for the team (something appropriate for the student's age and functioning level). The principal should be alerted so he or she can drop in. Other family members may be able to join the occasion. The whole point of the gathering is to acknowledge the progress the student has made and particularly to acknowledge and underscore the role the parents have played in contributing to the progress. If gatherings are not practical, send home special notes or make an extra call to acknowledge the accomplishments that are shared by all. There is nothing like celebrating success to solidify partnerships and to provide encouragement to all team members.

Step 9: Provide Professional Support to Parents

Just as there is a wide range in the needs of students with ASD (as the term *spectrum* implies), there is also a wide range in needs of the parents of these students. Some parents are very well informed about ASD and seek ongoing updates and support. Other parents are not so informed and barely have a rudimentary knowledge base of ASD. Given this range of needs, teachers can be a useful resource to parents.

For parents who are just getting started in their efforts to better understand ASD, provide basic information in the form of readily available pamphlets, short articles, and parent-friendly books. A short list of these materials is presented in Box 10.1: Basic Information for Parents on ASD.

| Box 10.1 | Basic Information for Parents on ASD |

> Grandin, T. (2011). *The Way I See It: A Personal Look at Autism and Asperger's* (2nd ed.). Arlington, TX: Future Horizons.
>
> Sicile-Kira, C. (2004). *Autism Spectrum Disorders: The Complete Guide to Understanding Autism, Asperger's Syndrome, Pervasive Developmental Disorder, and Other ASDs.* New York, NY: Perigree Books.
>
> Volkmar, F. R., & Weisner, L. A. (2009). *A Practical Guide to Autism: What Every Parent, Family Member, and Teacher Needs to Know.* Hoboken, NJ: John Wiley & Sons.

Other parents are well informed on the basics of ASD and need more, or more current, information that is focused on research and current best practices. It is also important for teachers and the team to be reasonably informed on current research and best practices regarding ASD for their own responsibilities and to be in a position to assist parents. Some recommended resources along these lines are listed in Box 10.2: Resources for Parents Seeking Additional Information on ASD.

| Box 10.2 | Resources for Parents Seeking Additional Information on ASD |

> *Focus on Autism and Other Developmental Disabilities.* http://foa.sage pub.com
>
> Heflin, L. J. (2007). *Students With Autism Spectrum Disorders: Effective Instructional Practices.* Upper Saddle River, NJ: Pearson/Merrill Prentice Hall.
>
> Simpson, R. L. (2005). *Autism Spectrum Disorders: Intervention and Treatments for Children and Youth.* Thousand Oaks, CA: Corwin.
>
> Whitman, T. L., & DeWitt, N. (2011). *Key Learning Skills for Children With Autism Spectrum Disorders: A Blueprint for Life.* Philadelphia, PA: Jessica Kingsley.

Teachers can also play an important role in helping parents evaluate the multiple practices or approaches that are being promoted in the field. Some of these practices have a solid research or evidence base. Others are unsupported fads or gimmicks that are promoted to unsuspecting parents. Parents of students with ASD who have meltdowns are often desperate for help and relief and are looking for the miracle cure for their child. They can become prey for the promoters of highly questionable practices.

As the teacher develops a strong collaborative relationship with the parents of a child with ASD who exhibits challenging behaviors, the parents may feel comfortable enough to share with the teacher other approaches that they are interested in using—some of which may be of questionable effectiveness and may even be detrimental to the child in the long run. Or the parents may ask the teacher's opinion about a given technique or approach. In these cases direct the parents to the variety of resources available to them to help them become better informed about different therapies and treatments. Some of these resources are listed in Box 10.3: Resources for Evaluating ASD Programs.

Box 10.3	Resources for Evaluating ASD Programs

Association for Science in Autism Treatment, *Summaries of Scientific Research on Interventions in Autism:* www.asatonline.org

Healing Thresholds: www.healingthresholds.com

Interactive Autism Network: www.iancommunity.org

Simpson, R. L. (2005). *Autism Spectrum Disorders: Intervention and Treatments for Children and Youth.* Thousand Oaks, CA: Corwin.

For example, parents may have come across *pet therapy* as a way of helping to calm their child. The parents see merit in this approach, knowing that pets have a calming effect on adults and children in general. So the parents ask the teacher's opinion. In this situation, you would meet with the parents; gather critical information from their list of resources, such as those in in Box 10.3; identify the pros and cons of the approach and guidelines for its use; and make a determination on whether or not to use the strategy.

Step 10: Develop Home-Based
Component of Behavior Support Plan

We have tried to stress that it is especially advantageous, even necessary, for teachers and parents to collaborate in a strong partnership in order to effectively address meltdowns for students with ASD. In effect, both a school intervention and a home-based intervention need to be developed based on the same or highly similar approaches to ensure consistency for the student across school and home. We have described a six-phase model for depicting the meltdown cycle followed by procedures for developing a behavior support plan (Appendix B: Behavior Support Plan). In Chapter 9 behavior support plans based on this model were developed for two students, Ricky and Elena, in which the *assessment* and *strategies* components were completed (see Boxes 9.3 and 9.4). The parent component of Ricky's behavior support is now described. Ricky's situation is presented in Box 10.4: Case Study 1: Recap of Ricky's Behavioral History, followed by Box 10.5: Home-Based Behavior Support Plan for Ricky.

Box 10.4	Case Study 1: Recap of Ricky's Behavioral History

Ricky is a 5-year-old boy with autism. He never initiates conversations and rarely makes eye contact with other individuals. He has difficulty communicating with his peers and usually does not respond when people speak to him. On a regular basis, Ricky becomes upset and has serious meltdowns with screaming, throwing things around, rushing around the room, and flailing his arms. His parents report that his behavior at school and at home has worsened in that he is having more meltdowns since they moved to a different area of town and a new school. His parents reported that in his last meltdown at home, he was playing with a puzzle on his Game Boy, stopped for a while, and went to the closet as if to find something. He then slammed the closet door and started screaming and running around the room. He began to thrash on the floor and continued to scream. His mother asked the other children to play outside, and she cleared the center of the room of any objects near Ricky. She sat near him until he eventually calmed down. His mother then gave him the Game Boy, which he took and began to fiddle with, and after several minutes, he turned it on to begin playing a game.

Box 10.5	Home-Based Behavior Support Plan for Ricky

Student Name: Ricky Wiley   Date: 4/3/11

Teacher: Mary-Sharon Weatherspoon   Grade: 1

Staff Present: Josephine Wardley, Tom Scruggs, Ellen Hawthorne, and Mary-Sharon Weatherspoon

Parents Present: Rick and Athena Wiley

Assessment	*Strategies*
Calm	**Calm**
Plays by himself happily for up to 30 minutes	*Rearrange living/family room so he has his own space*
Let's me help him when assistance is needed	*Make some more visual cues and use frequently*
Can transition satisfactorily when finished with what he is doing	
Likes to be praised when he makes something	
Triggers	**Triggers**
Siblings start shouting or playing loudly	*Insist siblings and neighbors play quietly*
Neighbor children visiting siblings and playing loudly	*Show siblings and friends how to include him*
Stopping special interests for meals and bedtime	*Provide forewarning for meals and bedtime*
Denial of items at grocery store	*Prepare him for shopping—rehearse expected routines*
Agitation	**Agitation**
Ricky skips Phase III: Agitation and goes straight to Phase IV: Meltdown. In the background example he went to the closet and erupted into a meltdown.	*Presently not applicable*

Assessment	Strategies
Re-Grouping	**Re-Grouping**
Screaming began to subside, and he began to sit still on the floor.	*Sit near him, not too close but present so he knows you are there*
He accepted the Game Boy from his mother.	*Watch him to see when the screaming reduces and he stops thrashing on the floor, becoming quieter*
	Talk to him quietly
	Give him something he likes to play with, such as a Game Boy or computer game
	Allow him time to take it and play with it
Starting Over	**Starting Over**
He switched on the Game Boy and began to play with it again.	*Provide encouragement for settling down and playing the game*
	Comment on the game he is playing, and take a turn if appropriate
	Maintain supportive measures

Note: Each of these steps is discussed with the parents and clearly explained by the teacher (using the example from Box 10.4).

Chapter Summary

Students with ASD who exhibit meltdown behavior typically have serious problems in all the major settings of their lives—school, home, and the community. Each of these environments needs to be targeted in order to effectively change the student's behavior. This means that the parents play a critical role in not only contributing to the behavior support plan for school but also developing and implementing a plan tailored for the home and community. The development of these components in a comprehensive plan requires parents and educators to work together in a collaborative and reciprocal fashion whereby teachers and parents can learn from each other and support each other. Both parties benefit from this partnership. Teachers not only learn more about their student who has meltdowns but also come to a deeper appreciation of the critical role that the parents play in the life of the student. Parents have a wealth of information that they can share if they feel comfortable with and respected by the teachers. Parents also benefit from the expertise that the teachers provide in terms of helping them understand the processes involved with meltdown behavior in particular and ASD in general.

However, there are a number of factors that can inhibit effective parent-teacher partnerships that need to be effectively addressed. Moreover, teachers must take several steps to ensure that a strong working relationship is developed between themselves and the parents. The key message in these steps is that parents need to experience that they are critical members of the team in both planning and implementing the behavior support plan for their child. The parent role is an essential component.

Closing Remarks

There is no question: It is indisputable that students with autism spectrum disorder (ASD) face incredible challenges in all areas of life at school, at home, and in the community. They have unique deficits that substantially impact their learning and success at school, specifically their overreactivity to sensory conditions, problems with language and communication, difficulties with understanding and cognition in general, and socialization competence.

On top of these seemingly overwhelming limitations, some students with ASD experience an additional debilitating problem known in the field as a *meltdown*. This class of behavior often involves screaming, yelling, loud perseveration in speech; physical excesses such as flailing arms and hands, thrashing on the floor, and pounding on walls; and in some cases aggression toward others and self-abuse. Moreover, these episodes can last for considerable amounts of time, sometimes up to several hours. These situations are severely stressful for the student as well as for the teachers and parents. Both teachers and parents have reported that they are often unable to identify what it is specifically that triggers the meltdowns and are at a loss in terms of how to stop the episodes once they are in full flight. In fact, they have said that the strategies they have found effective with other students or other children not only do not work but exacerbate the problems.

The purpose of this book is to provide teachers and support personnel in schools with a model for describing the meltdown behaviors in terms of a behavioral cycle. The model depicts meltdowns in terms of six identifiable phases—Calm, Triggers, Agitation, Meltdowns, Re-Grouping, and Starting Over. The basic assumption is that the student starts out relatively calm and can function reasonably well in school given the constraints of the disability of ASD. Certain triggers come into play that are usually related to sensory overload, disruption of routines and surprises, and skill deficits in the areas of communication, cognition, and socialization. These triggers cause the student to become upset and usually move the student from the Calm Phase to the Agitation Phase in the cycle. If the triggers persist or new triggers arise, either externally or internally the student will accelerate to the Meltdown Phase. Over time the student will begin to settle to some extent from the meltdown and enter the transition phase of Re-Grouping and with further settling will resume the normal classroom activities for the final phase, Starting Over. However, if the same triggers are still present, or new ones emerge, then it is only a matter of time before the cycle starts up again and the student heads to another meltdown.

The main use of this model is to help teachers and parents pinpoint specific behaviors that the student engages in for each of the six phases. Time-tested classroom- and home-based strategies can then be applied to each phase. The overall value of this process is that once certain behaviors are exhibited for a specific phase, teachers and parents can implement corresponding strategies for that phase. The goal in using the model is to arrest the behavior at that point and prevent a meltdown or, if following a meltdown, help the student recover.

The model lends itself to developing a behavior support plan for the student with ASD who has meltdowns. A two-column form is used. In the first column, *Assessment,* the specific behaviors for each of the six phases are recorded, based on consensus from staff who work with the student. In the second column, *Strategies,* specific strategies appropriate for each phase are listed. In this way, for each phase behavioral indicators are listed along with corresponding strategies to be applied when the behavioral indicators are observed. It is understood that with this population, the term *spectrum* is used to capture the range in skill levels and variations in behavioral indicators and responsiveness to the various strategies. The implication is that the information provided in this book cannot be readily applied to a given student. Teachers and parents will have to search to find which specific strategies are most effective for the particular student. Hopefully, what is presented in this book will serve as a useful guideline for this search.

The behavior support plan also has a parent component. This book strongly encourages working effectively with parents as there are clear benefits to parents and teachers in establishing a strong parent-teacher partnership. Parents and teachers contribute to both the *Assessment* and *Strategies* sections of the behavior support plan. The outcome of such collaboration is a behavior support plan that has a component to be implemented at school and another component, the parent component, to be implemented in the home and community. Parents and teachers work closely together in both developing and implementing the plan in each environment.

Teachers and parents are to be admired for their persistence and dedication to this incredibly high-needs group of students who have to not only deal with the difficulties associated with ASD but also cope with the severe experiences and effects of meltdowns. There is still so much yet to be learned: What exactly is going on with the internalization of sensory overloading and other specific triggers that lead to meltdowns? What internal processing is happening during the course of a meltdown? How can teachers and parents effectively reach the student when a meltdown is underway? Meanwhile, teachers and parents must deal with the students without solid answers to these questions. We hope that the model developed in this book is useful in helping teachers and parents chart the cycle of meltdowns, intervene accordingly, and provide these students with the level of support they so desperately need in their education and in their home life.

Appendices

Appendix A. Summary and Checklist for Behaviors of Each Phase in the Meltdown Cycle (Form 3.1)

StudentName:_____   Date:_____

Teacher: _____   Grade: _____

Phase I: Calm

Overall, behavior is cooperative, focused, and acceptable.

☐ Maintains on-task behavior
☐ Engages in tasks and activities
☐ Follows directions
☐ Permits assistance
☐ Makes transitions successfully
☐ Responds to praise and positive interactions
☐ Initiates requests and interactions
☐ Other

Phase II: Triggers

Overall, student has trouble with understanding and communicating.

☐ Disruption of schedules and routines
☐ Sensory overload or cravings
☐ Inability to communicate needs
☐ Inability to understand
☐ Conflicts
☐ Pressure
☐ Ineffective problem solving
☐ Facing correction procedures
☐ Motor skill activities
☐ Impact of health issues
☐ Spillover from health issues from home
☐ Other

(Continued)

(Continued)

Phase III: Agitation

Overall, student exhibits sudden increases or decreases in behavior.

Increases in Behavior	Decreases in Behavior
☐ Busy hands and feet	☐ Staring into space
☐ Repetitive self-talk	☐ Veiled eyes
☐ Increases in self-stimulation	☐ Becoming mute
☐ Low-level destructive behaviors	☐ Contained hands
☐ Changes in body language	☐ Withdrawing from activity
☐ Aimless pacing and wandering	☐ Seeking isolation
☐ Cognitive breakdowns	☐ Other
☐ Stuttering	
☐ Noncompliance	
☐ Whining, making noises, and crying	
☐ Other	

Phase IV: Meltdown

Overall, behavior is out of control.

☐ Serious destruction of property
☐ Physical attacks
☐ Self-abuse
☐ Severe tantrums
☐ Running away
☐ Other

Phase V: Re-Grouping

Overall, student withdraws and displays confusion.

☐ Withdrawal
☐ Confusion
☐ Reconciliation attempts
☐ Denial
☐ Responsiveness to directions
☐ Responsiveness to manipulative or mechanical tasks
☐ Responsiveness to special interests

☐ Avoidance of discussion
☐ Limited coordination
☐ Other

Phase VI: Starting Over

Overall, student is responsive to concrete tasks and reluctant to interact.

☐ Eagerness for independent work or activity
☐ Subdued behavior in group work
☐ Subdued behavior in class discussions
☐ Defensive behavior
☐ Cautious with problem solving
☐ Increased focus
☐ Increased physical calm
☐ Other

Source: Adapted from Colvin, 2004.

Appendix B. Behavior Support Plan (Form 3.2)

Student Name: _____ Date: _____

Homeroom Teacher: _____ Grade: _____

Staff Present: _____

Assessment	Strategies
Calm	Calm
Triggers	Triggers
Agitation	Agitation
Meltdown	Meltdown
Re-Grouping	Re-Grouping
Starting Over	Starting Over

Appendix C. Organization of Classroom Space (Form 4.1)

Activity	Completion Date	Notes
1. Locate specific classroom areas for:		
a. Independent work	__/__/__	_____
b. Group work	__/__/__	_____
c. Choice activities	__/__/__	_____
d. Quiet time	__/__/__	_____
e. Time-out or isolation	__/__/__	_____
f. Storage materials and supplies	__/__/__	_____
g. Teacher's desk	__/__/__	_____
h. Notice board	__/__/__	_____
i. Remove obstructions to supervision	__/__/__	_____
j. Other	__/__/__	
2. Design flexible seating arrangements:		
a. Rows	__/__/__	_____
b. Clusters	__/__/__	_____
c. Semicircular	__/__/__	_____
d. Combinations	__/__/__	_____
e. Other		
3. Identify other classroom design tasks and functions		
_____	__/__/__	_____
_____		_____
_____		_____
_____		_____

Appendix D. Checklist of Adjustments for Sensory Issues (Form 4.2)

Sensory Issue	Adjustment Options	Date Completed	Notes
Auditory	Reduce classroom noise Use headphones Develop quiet area Prepare student Other	__/__/__	
Visual	Use dimmers Reduce lighting Reduce visual distraction Other	__/__/__	
Tactile	Control congestion areas Minimize high-traffic areas Locate student's desk in low-traffic area Be aware of touching issues	__/__/__	
Gustatory	Identify preferred foods Offer choices for snacks Offer menu for lunch	__/__/__	

Sensory Issue	Adjustment Options	Date Completed	Notes
Olfactory	Monitor and reduce body scents, aftershave lotions, perfumes, and colognes Provide small fan Seat student near open window Be aware of scented supplies (stickers, etc.)	___/___/___	
Proprioceptive and Vestibular	Develop plan with occupational therapist Use rocking chair and mini-trampoline Provide physical space	___/___/___	
Other Sensory	Monitor temperature	___/___/___	

198

Appendix E. Steps for Developing a Visual Support System (Form 4.3)

Student Level: _____

Step 1: Identify areas of the school day where visual supports are needed

Step 2: Select the type of visuals to be used

Step 3: Collect the needed symbols

Step 4: Create and package the visual supports to be used

Appendix F. Plan for Teaching Classroom Expectations to Elementary Students (Form 4.4)

Expected Behavior: _____

Student Level: _____

Step 1: Explain

Student With ASD:

Step 2: Specify student behaviors

Student With ASD:

Step 3: Practice

Student With ASD:

Step 4: Monitor

Student With ASD:

Step 5: Review

Student With ASD:

Appendix G. Plan for Teaching Classroom Expectations to Secondary Students (Form 4.5)

Expected Behavior: _____

Student Level: _____

Step 1: Remind

Student With ASD:

Step 2: Supervise

Student With ASD:

Step 3: Provide feedback

Student With ASD:

Appendix H. Checklist and Action Plan for Defusing Agitation (Form 6.1)

Strategy	Action
1. Know the student	
2. Assess teacher or adult response	
3. Develop understanding	
4. Use empathy	
5. Help the student focus	
6. Provide space	
7. Provide assurances and additional time	
8. Permit special interest activities	
9. Schedule buffer breaks	
10. Use teacher proximity	
11. Schedule independent activities	
12. Employ passive activities	
13. Use movement activities	
14. Use self-management approaches when appropriate	
15. Establish relaxation centers	
16. Provide physical contact as appropriate	

Appendix I. Checklist and Action Plan for Pre-Requisite Steps in Managing Meltdowns (Form 7.1)

Student Level:		
Step	*Date*	*Action*
Step 1: Obtain parent approval	__/__/__	
Step 2: Arrange professional preparation for staff	__/__/__	
Step 3: Arrange preparation for office staff and administration	__/__/__	
Step 4: Follow school policies and the IEP	__/__/__	
Step 5: Ensure classroom and schoolwide readiness	__/__/__	
Step 6: Prepare the students	__/__/__	

Appendix J. Incident Report for a Meltdown (Form 7.2)

Incident Report

Student Name _____ Grade _____ Date _____

Written by _____ Classroom teacher _____

Staff member initially involved _____

Staff member managing incident _____

Start time of incident _____ End time _____ Duration _____

Report of any injuries sustained: _____

_____

_____

_____

Initial steps taken by staff member: _____

_____

_____

_____

List of possible triggers: _____

_____

_____

_____

(Continued)

(Continued)

List of agitation signs: _____

_____

_____

_____

Behaviors during meltdown: _____

_____

_____

_____

_____

Responses by staff member during meltdown: _____

_____

_____

_____

_____

Transition stages from meltdown to recovery: _____

_____

_____

_____

_____

Additional steps taken:

Parent contact _____ Meeting called _____ Other _____

Appendix K. Checklist and Action Plan for Intervention Steps in Managing a Meltdown (Form 7.3)

Student Level:	
Step	*Action*
Step 1: Guide the student to the safe place	
Step 2: Implement supportive measures	
Step 3: Manage more than one meltdown at a time (as needed)	
Step 4: Identify signs of meltdown recovery	
Step 5: Document the meltdown incident	

Appendix L. Probes for the Re-Grouping Phase Across Spectrum Levels (Form 8.1)

Level in Spectrum	Initial Probes	Expanded Probes
Lower Level		
Mid-Level		
Upper Level		

Appendix M. Checklist and Action Plan for Re-Grouping Phase (Form 8.2)

Student Level:
Stage 1: Present single-step interactions
Stage 2: Expand the interaction tasks
Stage 3: Exit to a preferred activity in the classroom
Stage 4: Enter the scheduled classroom activity

Appendix N. Checklist and Action Plan for Starting Over (Form 9.1)

Student Level:
Step 1: Provide strong emphasis on scheduled activities
Step 2: Focus on scheduled transitions
Step 3: Develop a debriefing plan
Step 4: Shape sensory reactions
Step 5: Heighten emphasis on skill building
Step 6: Develop behavior support plan

References

Abramson, R. K., Ravan, S. A., Wright, H. H., Wiediwult, K., Wolpert, C. M., Donnelly, S. A., . . . Cuccaro, M. L. (2005). The relationship between restrictive and repetitive behaviors in individuals with autism and obsessive compulsive symptoms in parents. *Child Psychiatry and Human Development, 36,* 155–165.

American Psychiatric Association. (2000). *Diagnostic and statistical manual of mental disorders* (4th ed., Text rev.). Washington, DC: Author.

American Psychiatric Association. (2010). *Proposed revisions.* Retrieved from http://www.dsm5.org/proposedrevision/Pages/Default.aspx

Arick, J., Loos, L., Falco, R., & Krug, D. (2005). *The STAR program: Strategies for teaching based on autism research.* Austin, TX: Pro-Ed.

Aspy, R., & Grossman, B. G. (2008). *Designing comprehensive interventions for individuals with high-functioning autism and Asperger syndrome: The Ziggurat model.* Overland Park, KS: Autism Asperger.

Attwood, T. (2007). *The complete guide to Asperger's syndrome.* London, UK: Jessica Kingsley.

Baker, J. E. (2003). *Social skills training for children and adolescents with Asperger syndrome and related social communication disorders.* Shawnee Mission, KS: Autism Asperger.

Belfiore, P. J., Pulley Basile, S., & Lee, D. L. (2008). Using a high probability command sequence to increase classroom compliance: The role of behavioral momentum. *Journal of Behavioral Education, 17,* 160–171.

Bialer, D. S., & Miller, L. J. (2011). *No longer a secret: Unique common sense strategies for children with sensory or motor challenges.* Arlington, TX: Sensory World.

Bodfish, J. W., Symons, F. J., Parker, D. E., & Lewis, M. H. (2000). Varieties of repetitive behavior in autism: Comparisons to mental retardation. *Journal of Autism and Developmental Disorders, 30,* 237–243.

Bogdashina, O. (2003). *Sensory perceptual issues in autism and Asperger syndrome.* London, UK: Jessica Kingsley.

Brophy, J. (1999). Toward a model of the value aspects of motivation in education: Developing appreciation for particular learning domains and activities. *Educational Psychologist, 34*(2), 75–85.

Buie, T., Campbell, D. B., Fuchs, G. J., Furuta, G. T., Levy, J., Vandewater, J., . . . Winter, H. (2010). Evaluation, diagnosis, and treatment of gastrointestinal disorders in individuals with ASD: A consensus report. *Pediatrics, 125,* S1–S18.

Carter, E., Sisco, L. G., Chung, Y., & Stanton-Chapman, T. (2010). Peer interactions of students with intellectual disabilities and/or autism: A map of the intervention literature. *Research & Practice for Persons With Severe Disabilities, 35*(3–4), 63–79.

Cates, G. L., & Dalenberg, A. E. (2005). Effects of interspersing rate on student preferences for mathematics assignments. *Journal of Behavioral Education, 14,* 89–104.

Centers for Disease Control and Prevention. (2009). Prevalence of autism spectrum disorders—Autism and Developmental Disabilities Monitoring Network, United States, 2006. Surveillance summaries. *Morbidity and Mortality Weekly Report, 58*(No. SS-10).

Cohen, M. J., & Sloan, D. L. (2007). *Visual supports for people with autism: A guide for parents and professionals.* Bethesda, MD: Woodbine House.

Colvin, G. (1999). *Defusing anger and aggression: Safe strategies for secondary school educators* [DVD]. Eugene, OR: IRIS Media.

Colvin, G. (2002). Designing classroom organization and structure. In K. L. Lane, F. M. Gresham, & T. E. O'Shaughnessy (Eds.), *Interventions for children with or at risk or emotional and behavioral disorder* (pp. 159–174). Boston, MA: Allyn & Bacon.

Colvin, G. (2004). *Managing the cycle of acting-out behavior in the classroom.* Eugene, OR: Behavior Associates.

Colvin, G. (2005). Precorrection: Anticipating problem behavior. In M. Hersen, G. Sugai, & R. Horner (Eds.), *Encyclopedia of behavior modification and cognitive behavior therapy* (Vol. 3, pp. 1437–1441). Thousand Oaks, CA: Sage.

Colvin, G. (2007). *7 steps for developing a proactive schoolwide discipline plan: A guide for principals and leadership teams.* Thousand Oaks, CA: Corwin.

Colvin, G. (2010). *Defusing disruptive behavior in the classroom.* Thousand Oaks, CA: Corwin.

Colvin, G., & Lazar, M. (1997). *The effective elementary classroom: Managing for success.* Longmont, CO: Sopris West.

Colvin, G., Sugai, G., & Patching, W. (1993). Pre-correction: An instructional approach for managing predictable problem behavior. *Intervention in School and Clinic, 28,* 143–150.

Commons, M. L., & White, M. S. (2003). A complete theory of tests for a theory of mind must consider hierarchical complexity and stage. *Behavioral and Brain Sciences, 26,* 606–607.

Cotton, K. (2003). *Principals and student achievement: What the research says.* Alexandria, VA: Association for Supervision and Curriculum Development.

Crisis Prevention Institute. (2011). *Nonviolent crisis intervention.* Retrieved from http://www.crisisprevention.com/Specialties/Nonviolent-Crisis-Intervention

Darch, C., & Kame'enui, E. J. (2004). *Instructional classroom management: A proactive approach to classroom management* (2nd ed.). Upper Saddle River, NJ: Pearson Education.

Earles-Vollrath, T. L., Tapscott Cook, K., & Ganz, J. B. (2006). *How to develop and implement visual supports.* Austin, TX: Pro-Ed.

Engelmann, S., & Carnine, D. (1991). *Theory of instruction.* Eugene, OR: Association for Direct Instruction.

Flores, M. M., & Ganz, J. B. (2007). Effectiveness of direct instruction for teaching statement inference, use of facts, and analogies to students with developmental disabilities and reading delays. *Focus on Autism and Other Developmental Disabilities, 22*, 244–251.

Flores, M. M., & Ganz, J. B. (2009). The effects of direct instruction on the reading comprehension of students with autism and developmental disabilities. *Education and Training in Developmental Disabilities, 44*(1), 39–53.

Fournier, K. A., Hass, C. J., Naik, S. F., Lodha, N., & Cauraugh, J. H. (2010). Motor coordination in autism spectrum disorders: A synthesis and meta-analysis. *Journal of Autism and Developmental Disorders, 40*, 1227–1240.

Frase, L., & Hetzel, R. (1990). *School management by wandering around.* Lancaster, PA: Technomic.

Frith, U. (Ed.). (1991). *Autism and Asperger syndrome.* Cambridge, UK: University Press.

Gadaire, D. M., Kelley, M. E., & DeRosa, N. M. (2010). Research needed for focusing on additional generality of applied behavior analysis. *Behavior Analyst Today, 11*, 49–58.

Ganz, J. (2007). Classroom structuring methods and strategies for children and youth with autism spectrum disorders. *Exceptionality, 15*, 249–260.

Goldstein, H. S., Johnson-Martin, N., Goldman, B. D., & Hussey, B. (1992). Object play and exploration in children with and without disabilities: A longitudinal study. *American Journal on Mental Retardation, 97*, 21–38.

Grandin, T. (2011). *The way I see it: A personal look at autism and Asperger's* (2nd ed.). Arlington, TX: Future Horizons.

Gresham, F., & Kern, L. (2004). Internalizing behavior problems in children and adolescents. In R. Rutherford, M. Quinn, & S. Mathur (Eds.), *Handbook of research in emotional and behavioral disorders* (pp. 262–281). New York, NY: Guilford Press.

Handle With Care: Behavior management system. (n.d.). Retrieved from http://handlewithcare.com

Heflin, L. J. (2007). *Students with autism spectrum disorders: Effective instructional practices.* Upper Saddle River, NJ: Pearson/Merrill Prentice Hall.

Hogdon, L. A. (1995). *Visual strategies for improving communication: Practical supports for school and home.* Troy, MI: QuirkRoberts.

Hogdon, L. A. (1999). *Solving behavior problems in autism: Improving communication with visual strategies.* Troy, MI: QuirkRoberts.

Holm, O. (1997). Ratings of empathic communication: Does experience make a difference? *Journal of Psychology, 3*, 680–689.

Ingersoll, B., & Dvortcsak, A. (2010). *Teaching social communication to children with autism: A practitioner's guide to parent training.* New York, NY: Guilford Press.

Ingersoll, R., & Smith, T. (2003). The wrong solution to the teacher shortage. *Educational Leadership, 60*(8), 30–33.

Kauffman, J. M., Mostert, M. P., Trent, S. C., & Hallahan, D. E. (1998). *Managing classroom behavior: A reflective case-based approach* (2nd ed.). Boston, MA: Allyn & Bacon.

Kern, L., & Clemens, N. H. (2005). Task interspersal. In M. Hersen, G. Sugai, & R. Horner (Eds.), *Encyclopedia of behavior modification and cognitive behavior therapy* (Vol. 3, pp. 1565–1568). Thousand Oaks, CA: Sage.

Kern, L., Hilt, A. M., & Gresham, F. (2004). Functional assessment for students with or at risk for emotional and behavioral disorders: A review. *Education and Treatment of Children, 27*, 440–452.

Kern, L., & Starosta, K. M. (2004). Behavioral momentum. In M. Hersen, G. Sugai, & R. Horner (Eds.), *Encyclopedia of behavior modification and cognitive behavior therapy* (Vol. 3, pp. 1189–1190). Thousand Oaks, CA: Sage.

Kluth, P. (2009). *The autism checklist: A practical reference for parents and teachers.* San Francisco, CA: Jossey-Bass.

Kranowitz, C. S. (2005). *The out-of-sync child: Recognizing and coping with sensory processing disorder.* New York, NY: Perigee.

Krebs, M. L., McDaniel, D. M., & Neeley, R. A. (2010). The effects of peer training on the social interactions of children with autism spectrum disorders. *Education, 13*, 393–403.

Lecavalier, L., Leone, S., & Wiltz, J. (2006). The impact of behavior problems on caregiver stress in young people with autism spectrum disorders. *Journal of Intellectual Disability Research, 50*, 172–183.

Lipsky, D., & Richards, W. (2009). *Managing meltdowns: Using the S.C.A.R.E.D. calming technique with children and adults with autism.* Philadelphia, PA: Jessica Kingsley.

Maag, J. W. (2004). *Behavior management: From theoretical implications to practical applications* (2nd ed.). Belmont, CA: Wadsworth/Thompson Learning.

Machalicek, W., O'Reilly, M. F., Beretvas, N., Sigafoos, J., & Lancioni, G. E. (2007). A review of interventions to reduce challenging behavior in school settings for students with autism spectrum disorders. *Research in Autism Spectrum Disorders, 1*, 229–246.

Malow, B. A., Marzec, M. L., McGrew, S. G., Wang, L., Henderson, L. M., & Stone, W. L. (2006). Characterizing sleep in children with autism spectrum disorders: A multidimensional approach. *Sleep, 29*, 1563–1571.

Matson, J. L., & Nebel-Schwalm, M. (2007). Assessing challenging behaviors in children with autism spectrum disorders: A review. *Research in Developmental Disabilities, 28*, 567–579.

McClannahan, L. E., & Krantz, P. J. (2010). *Activity schedules for children with autism: Teaching independent behavior* (2nd ed.). Bethesda, MD: Woodbine House.

Mesibov, G., & Howley, M. (2003). *Accessing the curriculum for pupils with autism spectrum disorders: Using the TEACCH Programme to help inclusion.* London, UK: David Fulton.

Ming, X., Brimacombe, M., & Wagner, G. C. (2007). Prevalence of motor impairment in autism spectrum disorders. *Brain Development, 29*, 565–570.

Minshew, N. J., & Goldstein, G. (1998). Autism as a disorder of complex information processing. *Mental Retardation and Developmental Disabilities Research Reviews, 4*, 129–136.

Molloy, C. A., Dietrich, K. N., & Bhattacharya, A. (2003). Postural stability in children with autism spectrum disorder. *Journal of Autism and Developmental Disorders, 33*, 643–652.

Moran, C., Stobbe, J. C., Baron, W., Miller, J., & Moir, E. (2008). *Keys to the elementary classroom: A new teacher's guide to the first month of school* (3rd ed.). Thousand Oaks, CA: Corwin.

Moyes, R. A. (2002). *Addressing the challenging behavior of children with high-functioning autism/Asperger syndrome in the classroom.* Philadelphia, PA: Jessica Kingsley.

Murray-Slutsky, C., & Paris, B. A. (2005). *Is it sensory or is it behavior? Behavior problem identification, assessment, and intervention.* Austin, TX: Hammill Institute on Disabilities.

National Research Council, Committee on Educational Interventions for Children with Autism. (2001). *Educating children with autism.* Washington, DC: National Academy Press.

Neff, K. (2011). *Self-compassion: Stop beating yourself up and leave insecurity behind.* New York, NY: HarperCollins.

NAPPI International. (2009). *NAPPI resource center.* Retrieved from http://www.nappi-training.com/category/4956/nappi-resource-center.htm

Novak, G., & Pelaez, M. (2011). Autism: A behavioral systems approach. In E. A. Mayville & J. A. Mullick (Eds.), *Behavioral foundations of effective autism treatment* (pp. 13–33). Cornwall-on-Hudson, NY: Sloan.

Oliver, R. M., & Reschly, D. J. (2007). *Effective classroom management: Teacher preparation and professional development.* Washington, DC: Learning Point Associates, National Center on Teacher Quality.

Osborne, L. A., & Reed, P. (2009). The relationship between parenting stress and behavior problems of children with Autistic Spectrum Disorders. *Exceptional Children, 76,* 54–73.

Owen-DeSchryver, J. S., Carr, E. G., Cale, S. I., & Blakely-Smith, A. (2008). Promoting social interactions between students with autism spectrum disorders and their peers in inclusive school settings. *Focus on Autism and Other Developmental Disabilities, 23,* 15–28.

Ozonoff, S., Young, G. S., Goldring, S., Greiss-Hess, L., Herrera, A. M., Steele, J., . . . Rogers, S. J. (2008). Gross motor development, movement abnormalities, and early identification of autism. *Journal of Autism and Developmental Disorders, 38,* 644–656.

Pelaez-Nogueras, M. (1996). Multiple influences in behavioral interactions. *Behavioral Development Bulletin, 2,* 10–14.

Rogers, S. J., & Ozonoff, S. (2005). Annotation: What do we know about sensory dysfunction in autism? A critical review of the evidence. *Journal of Child Psychology and Psychiatry, 46,* 1255–1286.

Schieve, L. A., Blumberg, S. J., Rice, C., Visser, S. N., & Boyle, C. (2007). The relationship between autism and parenting stress. *Pediatrics, 119,* 114–121.

Schrandt, J. A., Buffington, D., & Poulson, C. L. (2009). Teaching empathy skills to children with autism. *Journal of Applied Behavior Analysis, 42,* 17–32.

Scull, J., & Winkler, A. M. (2011). *Shifting trends in special education.* Washington, DC: Thomas B. Fordham Institute.

Sicile-Kira, C. (2004). *Autism spectrum disorders: The complete guide to understanding autism, Asperger's syndrome, pervasive developmental disorder, and other ASDs.* New York, NY: Perigee Books.

Simpson, R. L. (2005). *Autism spectrum disorders: Intervention and treatments for children and youth.* Thousand Oaks, CA: Corwin.

Smith Myles, B., & Southwick, J. (2005). *Asperger syndrome and difficult moments: Practical solutions for tantrums, rage, and meltdowns* (2nd ed.). Shawnee Mission, KS: Autism Asperger.

Sprague, J. R., & Golly, A. (2004). *Best behavior: Building positive behavior support in schools.* Longmont, CO: Sopris West Educational Services.

Sprick, R., & Garrison, M. (2008). *Interventions: Evidence-based behavioral strategies for individual students* (2nd ed.). Eugene, OR: Pacific Northwest.

Stein, M. T. (2007, March 21). The prevalence of autism spectrum disorders. *Journal Watch Pediatrics and Adolescent Medicine.* Retrieved from http://pediatrics.jwatch.org/cgi/content/full/2007/321/1

Stevens, M., Washington, A., Rice, C., Jenner, W., Ottolino, J., & Clancy, K. (2007). *Prevalence of autism spectrum disorders (ASDs) in multiple areas of the United States, 2000 and 2002.* Atlanta, GA: Centers for Disease Control and Prevention.

Szatmari, P., Georgiades, S., Bryson, S., Zwaigenbaum, L., Roberts, W., Mahoney, W., . . . Tuff, L. (2006). Investigating the structure of the restricted, repetitive behaviours and interest domains of autism. *Journal of Child Psychology and Psychiatry, 47,* 582–590.

Tager-Flusberg, H., Paul, R., & Lord, C. E. (2005). Language and communication in autism. In F. Volkmar, R. Paul, A. Klin, & D. J. Cohen (Eds.), *Handbook of autism and pervasive developmental disorder* (3rd ed., Vol. 1, pp. 335–364). New York: John Wiley & Sons.

Tehee, E., Honan, R., & Hevey, D. (2009). Factors contributing to stress in parents of individuals with autistic spectrum disorders. *Journal of Applied Research in Intellectual Disabilities, 22,* 34–42.

Thelen, E. (2008). Grounded in the world: Developmental origins of the embodied mind. In W. F. Overton, U. Muller, & J. L. Newman (Eds.), *Developmental perspective on embodiment and consciousness* (pp. 99–129). New York, NY: Lawrence Erlbaum.

Thelen, E., & Smith, L. (1996). *A dynamic systems approach to the development of perception and action.* Cambridge, MA: MIT Press.

Thiemann-Bourque, K. (2010, April 27). Navigating the transition to middle school: Peer network programming. *The ASHA Leader,* pp. 12–15.

Thompson, T. (2009). *Freedom from meltdowns: Dr. Thompson's solutions for children with autism.* Baltimore, MD: Paul Brookes.

Turner, M. (1999). Annotation: Repetitive behavior in autism: A review of the psychological research. *Journal of Child Psychology and Psychiatry, 40,* 839–849.

VanDerHeyden, A. M. (2005). Prompting. In M. Hersen, G. Sugai, & R. Horner (Eds.), *Encyclopedia of behavior modification and cognitive behavior therapy* (Vol. 3, pp. 1470–1471). Thousand Oaks, CA: Sage.

Volkmar, F. R., & Weisner, L. A. (2009). *A practical guide to autism: What every parent, family member, and teacher needs to know.* New York, NY: John Wiley & Sons.

Walker, H. M., Ramsey, E., & Gresham, F. M. (2003). *Antisocial behavior in schools: Evidence-based practices.* Florence, KY: Wadsworth/Cengage Learning.

White, S. W., Oswald, D., Ollendick, T., & Scahill, L. (2009). Anxiety in children and adolescents with autism spectrum disorders. *Clinical Psychology Review, 29,* 216–229.

Williams, D. L, Goldstein, G., & Minshew, N. J. (2006). Neurological functioning in children with autism: Further evidence for distorted complex information processing, *Child Neuropsychology, 12,* 279–298.

Williams, D. L., & Minshew, N. L. (2010, April 27). How the brain thinks in autism: Implications for language intervention. *The ASHA Leader,* pp. 8–11.

Williams, G. P., Sears, L. L., & Allard, A. (2004). Sleep problems in children with autism. *Journal of Sleep Research, 13,* 265–268.

Woodcock, L., & Page, A. (2010). *Managing family meltdown: The low arousal approach and autism.* London, UK: Jessica Kingsley.

Index